YOUR BREATH IS YOUR GURU

Also by Galen Pearl

10 Steps to Finding Your Happy Place
(and Staying There)

I Speak to All Just So

YOUR BREATH IS YOUR GURU

Galen Pearl

STILL CREEK PRESS

PORTLAND, OREGON

Your Breath Is Your Guru
Sill Creek Press, Portland, OR

© 2023 by Galen Pearl

Book design by Vinnie Kinsella, Paper Chain Book Publishing Services

ISBN: 978-0-9858462-5-1
eISBN: 978-0-9858462-6-8

to Margaret who taught me that water moves the color
and
to Kyle who taught me to trust the process

Contents

In this very moment
Is a doorway
Beyond that doorway
Is where we really are
And always have been
From there our spirit calls us to come home
Walk through the door
What you leave behind is only a dream
Do not fear to leave it
If you only knew what awaits you
You would leap laughing through the portal
And never look back

Introduction

I was walking with a friend, chatting about various things, when she turned to me and said, "You are my guru." I laughed and responded, "No, I'm not anyone's guru. Your breath is your guru."

It's true. And it's that simple.

My shelves are filled with books on spirituality, mysticism, happiness, meditation, religion, enlightenment, and more. I used to read them because I thought they held a secret, *the* secret, to all I ever wanted to know. I came to understand, however, that I would never find what I sought in those books, or in the workshops or retreats that I attended.

I would find what I sought only when I quit looking for it, when I realized that it was never lost. It is here, ever present, as close as every breath I take. And my breath, if I listen to its wisdom, will teach me everything I need to know.

We are conditioned from an early age to disregard our inner wisdom, to look outside ourselves for someone to tell us what is real, who we are, and how we should think and behave. Awakening isn't so much about attainment or acquisition, as it is about relinquishment of our dependence on what is outside of us, and letting go of everything that blocks our awareness. It's not about learning more, but rather unlearning what has gotten us stuck in mental structures of belief. It's about recognizing that we don't know what we think we know, and trusting the natural unfolding of our lives according to a rhythm and beauty that transcends our striving to control.

As we become more attuned with this inner guidance, we begin to live the experience of a life full of blessings, a life that dances to the music of all creation. And we expand into our destiny of oneness with all that is.

So why would you read this book after being told that you need no book to realize your soul's deepest longing? We all can use reminders now and then. And remembering takes some practice. I hope that is what this book is for you, a collection of reminders to practice remembering who you are. I hope that by reading it, you are empowered to give yourself permission to trust your inner guidance, the wisdom that speaks to all of us, linking us to each other and to our common breath of existence.

Perhaps by sharing some of the things I've learned along the way, you might recognize your own experience and know that you are among kindred souls, that we are all, in essence, kindred souls. You are not alone, ever, and you are always loved.

Every breath is Life's tender caress of love

<u>PART 1</u>

THE CALL
TO AWAKENING

CHAPTER 1

The Longing Soul

One night
When darkness made the edges soft
And thinned the veil
The boy wept
I miss home, he cried
We are home, his parents soothed
No, my home before, now sobbing
His parents stroked his back, perplexed
You mean our old house?
No, not that one, the one before!
There was no other
You were born in that house
No! he wailed. The one BEFORE!
His parents understood at last
And cried with him

Hearing the Call

The boy in the poem was young enough to remember where he came from, where we all come from. Home, the origin from which we all emerge into this manifested life. He heard the call of home. The boy is my friend's grandson, and it's no coincidence, I think, that his name is True.

Maybe you have experienced something like this too, although as we get older we might not be as aware of it. We might begin to sense an inner discomfort, a restlessness, a vague dissatisfaction. We want something. But what is it?

I know the feeling. Once I found myself with a full calendar, full of things that I wanted to do, that I usually enjoyed doing, but I wasn't enjoying them. Why not? I decided that it was worth finding out, so I cleared my calendar and waited to see what would happen. That's a lot of alone time with less distraction than usual. Unease was front and center in my awareness. What was causing this? My typical approach to such a question is to think about it. So I thought…and thought. But I got no answer, proving once again that thinking is highly overrated. Nothing seemed quite right, like when you're hungry and standing in front of the open refrigerator but nothing looks good.

Meanwhile, this undefined feeling was expanding, like a spring welling up and spreading over the ground, like a wave swelling as it rolls toward the shore. It was uncomfortable, mysterious, even slightly painful, and a little scary. But there was no escape. It was inside me, calling me, touching my heart, drawing me deep.

Longing. My soul was longing, as all souls do. We long for home, for awakening, for remembering who we are, for union. Like the instinct of salmon returning upstream from the sea to their spawning ground, this is the longing of creation to manifest into form and then return to the formlessness from which it emerges. As a wave is ever connected to the ocean from which it swells, so are we ever connected to our source. We are breathed into existence, ever sustained by and connected to the cosmic breath that speaks creation into being.

We long to feel again and always the embrace of the Love that birthed us, to know that we are whole and holy beings. We are all called home to our higher selves, to our one Self.

It is the call that all souls hear. The psalmist writes, "Deep calls to deep in the roar of your waterfalls." In the waterfall roar of our busy lives we often miss its quiet beckoning. But eventually, we all hear it, unmistakable and compelling.

We might resist for a while, wanting the familiarity of our distractions, the comfort of certainty, the safety of understanding. This longing of the soul brings none of those. It is a call back into mystery, unknown and unknowable. It can be unsettling, and exciting, and is ultimately irresistible. We hear it in the beat of our hearts, in the rhythm of our breath, in the silence of our souls. Deep calls to us, and sooner or later, what is deep within us answers.

Listen well to silence
Hear the crystal singing of your soul
The song of home
Calls all to come

What We Forgot

[We] are the sons and daughters
of Life's longing for itself.
~Khalil Gibran

We will discover that what we are longing for is not something out there, but our true nature, hidden within.

In 1954, an insignificant Buddha statue made of painted and decorated plaster was being moved from a modest shed in Bangkok to a new temple. Weighing over five tons, the statue was too heavy for the crane and it fell to the ground. The fall knocked a piece of plaster off the base. When the workers examined the damage they saw something shiny underneath. That something shiny turned out to be pure gold. Removing all the plaster revealed an exquisite, solid gold Buddha.

Crafted centuries before, the statue was at some point hidden under the plaster, probably to protect it from invaders. Over the years, the true nature of the statue was forgotten, and the plaster statue was at various times housed in minor temples and even stored in a tin shed.

Imagine everyone's surprise when they discovered the existence of this priceless treasure, which was revealed by simply removing the false exterior. When I lived in Bangkok, I stood before this gleaming statue, marveling at its breathtaking beauty. I marveled even more because of its story.

Its story is our story. Hidden under our exterior ego selves is our true nature, our gleaming, pure, divine perfection. We search high and low, reading books, following teachers, worshiping at altars, striving ever more diligently, more frantically, to find what we most desire. And all the while, it is right where it has always been, deep inside, waiting.

We have forgotten who we are. Like the people who believed for centuries that the plaster coating was the real statue, we have bought into the illusion that we are what we think ourselves to be, when in fact, we are more than our minds can possibly imagine or understand. But if we're lucky, at some point life will drop us on the ground, and a little piece of our carefully constructed protective layer will chip off. If we dare to peek inside, we will see the golden glow and inherent beauty of our true being.

The kingdom of God is within you.
~Luke 17:21

Ride or Die

As the deer pants for streams of water
so my soul pants for you, O God.
~Psalm 42:1

Eventually, the call to awaken becomes too compelling to ignore. A friend used to say that his prayer was "Whatever it takes." What he meant was that he would do anything to awaken, to open his heart ever wider to Love, to surrender ever more unreservedly to the Beloved, to fly ever more fearlessly into the all-consuming fire of the heart.

I was attracted to and repelled by his intensity of passion. Could one really live with such wild abandon? He seemed to. His life did not appear to be as crazy as his devotion sounded. I felt a bit like the restaurant customer in that famous scene in *When Harry Met Sally* where Meg Ryan faked an orgasm…you know the scene. The customer at a nearby table was mesmerized and told the server, "I'll have what she's having."

But do we really want it? I was chatting with my daughter about a situation involving my grandchildren when she paused and looked at me. "You're a ride or die Nana," she observed. A ride or die person is someone who will do anything for the one they love, no matter what. Of course, that made me laugh with respect to being a grandmother. But it also made me think about life and what we are willing to commit our whole selves to.

I've taken my friend's prayer and modified it as my favorite prayer for living an awakened life: "Whatever it takes…and please help me mean it." Because even in all my enthusiasm, there is a part that sometimes hesitates. What if whatever it takes is too much? And on some level I know the answer to that because what it takes is everything…and nothing. The price of awakening is giving up every illusion, every belief, every judgment, everything that separates us from each other and from sacred Oneness.

That doesn't sound like nothing. But from within the awakened embrace of the Beloved, everything that is not love is not real. All the grievances we nurse and cherish in the dark corners of our hearts disappear in the light of Truth. We wonder why we thought they were so important, if we remember them at all.

I don't know if I'm a ride or die Nana, but I want to be a ride or die human being. As I breathe my last breath, I want to smile and know that I left it all on the field. I held nothing back. I left not one day unloved. I embraced with infinite compassion all that arose in my sphere of experience. I lived showered in grace and bathed in gratitude. I surrendered every breath to the Beloved.

…and please help me mean it.

> *If you surrender to the wind you can ride it.*
> ~Toni Morrison

Riding the Wind

The wind that we surrender to and learn to ride is the wind of desire. Desire gets a bad rap in some spiritual traditions because it can lead us into attachment and suffering. But in its purest form, desire is the creative energy of the universe. Desire is the energy that generates form out of the undifferentiated formlessness of mystery. It is the movement of creation manifesting from, and returning to, stillness. It is beautiful and powerful.

The longing in our soul is the desire to heal the illusion of separation and to live in awakened awareness of our eternal union with all creation and the source of all creation. We need not fear it, but to ride the wind of desire requires mastery. This mastery is not domination or control, as in breaking or taming a wild horse. This is the mastery of surrender, becoming one with the generative power of the universe and riding it to our destiny. Riding it *is* our destiny.

Because we have been conditioned to resist desire lest we fall victim to it and be at its mercy, we have struggled with rather than embraced the very energy, the only energy, that will satisfy our soul's longing. Befriending such power, like befriending a wild horse, takes some practice, which we will explore more fully in Chapter 4.

But as a starting point, one thing you might notice is that the unskilled riding of the wind of desire can lead us on some detours.

For example, I once went to an informational introduction to a certain meditation method. However, as the presentation began, I realized that the information was being offered in the context of a sales pitch. The meditation method was the product being pitched, using slick power point slides and stage whispered suggestions of promised enlightenment which would benefit my life "in grand ways." The method was unique and far superior to anything in the same category, as evidenced by many scientific studies and personal testimonials. There was only one source for this product, and there was no way to "try out" the product until I paid for it. There was an aura of secret initiation, giving the buyer a sense of belonging to an elite group. I felt the pull even as I walked away.

The point is not whether this meditation method is beneficial. The point is that the sales pitch was geared to make the audience think that they lacked something essential to their spiritual growth and that only this organization could provide it. Desire in this context is a seductive emotion. It can take us on a wild goose chase by causing us distress that we believe can only be alleviated by obtaining the wanted object.

We all experience this. Even the Dalai Lama admits to a fondness for gadgets. He tells the story of walking by an electronics store and stopping to admire a device displayed in the window. Laughing, he described the desire that arose for this shiny object, even though he had no idea what the gadget was for.

Many of us can relate. Watching myself respond with at least curiosity if not outright craving to what I recognized as a marketing strategy...well, it sort of amazed me. What an opportunity to contemplate the nature of wanting. Wanting is not good or bad. It just is. We want some things; we don't want other things. But we needn't be at the mercy of our wanting. We can get to know it rather than blindly follow it. We can distinguish between desires in the mind that lead us astray, and desire of the soul that leads us home. And that knowing might benefit our lives in grand ways!

> *You are the face of my longing*
> *But you are not my longing*
> *You are the name of my longing*
> *But you are not my longing*
> *You are the form of my longing*
> *But you are not my longing*
> *You break my heart*
> *But it is not you*
> *It is my longing*

Getting More Acquainted with Desire

How is the longing of the soul for sacred union different from the "wanting" desire for things outside ourselves? Getting more acquainted with desire helps us learn to distinguish desire that guides us to our destiny from desire that distracts us and deludes us. Going more deeply into our experience of desire helps us learn to ride the wind rather than fighting with it.

Life gave me an opportunity to explore the nature of desire one day when I went for a walk and lost my house key along the way, as I discovered when I got back home and the key was not in my pocket. Mildly annoyed, I retraced my steps expecting to find it. But I didn't. Now annoyance was mixed with a growing sense of anxiety and discomfort, like the earth had suddenly and slightly shifted off its axis.

A neighbor who has a spare key to my house let me in, so the immediate problem was solved, but I was not at ease. Just a simple little key, right? On the contrary, that little key became the symbolic key to my well-being. I could not be at peace until I got it back. Every day I took the same walking route, eyes scanning the ground, willing it to appear. It did not.

I was self-aware enough to watch my distress with curiosity and not a little befuddlement. What could be so important about this key that I would sacrifice my equanimity? It's not like I didn't have other copies of my house key and could easily have as many copies as I wanted made at the hardware store. I couldn't explain the mystery of its crucial significance except to say that I wanted *that* key. I wanted it *a lot*.

That key clearly represented something far beyond its function of unlocking my front door. I had been struggling with a strong desire about something else at that same time, wanting certain things to be different than they were, wanting people to be different than they were, wanting myself to be different than I was. This desire was born of judgment and fantasy. Unlike the desire that calls us home, this desire brought pain and anger to my heart, sadness and distress to my emotions, and disquiet to my spirit.

I had shifted off my axis of balance and alignment. I wanted relief, not the relief that comes with familiar practices to restore equilibrium. No, I wanted the relief that we imagine we will experience if we get what we want, like the kid in the shopping basket screaming in the checkout line for the candy placed strategically just out of reach.

I know better … and yet …

Desire had a hold on me, not the desire of the soul for sacred awakening, but the desire of the mind wanting things to be different than they were. I was hooked and I knew it. I wasn't struggling with a lost key or unwanted circumstances as much as I was struggling with desire itself. I was judging it, rejecting it, denying it, pretending I didn't feel it, only to be caught up in its false promise of relief if I could just find that lost key. And even knowing that the promise was false, I wanted that key anyway.

But like with any intense emotion, you eventually wear out. So what can you do when you are too exhausted to struggle anymore? Surrender. I invited desire to tea and served my most delicious compassion. Desire still sits at the table of my thoughts, but it is calmer now, as am I. One sip at a time. One breath at a time.

When I run after what I think I want, my days are a
furnace of stress and anxiety. If I sit in my own place
of patience, what I need flows to me, and without
pain. From this I understand that what I want also
wants me, is looking for me, and attracting me. There
is a great secret here for anyone who can grasp it.
~Rumi

There Must Be a Better Way

As we explore our relationship with desire, especially when we are struggling with wanting things to be other than they are, it might occur to us that there must be a better way to master and ride the wind of desire. This thought that there must be a better way pops up in a myriad of contexts, and is often the genesis and the impetus for discoveries, inventions, and growth, for individuals, communities, and nations. It usually occurs to us when we are at the nadir of our efforts, energy, ideas. We are at an impasse, frustrated and flummoxed, exhausted by all the spiritual wild goose chases that have led nowhere. We remember the definition of insanity as doing the same thing over and over, thinking we will get a different result, and we recognize ourselves.

So we stop, momentarily empty.

That pause is what opens the door of the room that we have trapped ourselves in. Our inner light of golden Buddha nature shines always, reminding us that what we truly desire is to be who we truly are. We need only release everything that blocks the light of truth. The space created by release is what allows light to flood into the darkness of illusion that has imprisoned us. And into that light, the thought steps across the threshold: There must be a better way.

And in that moment, in our fatigue and despair, the spark of hope is ignited, and we are willing, if only for that moment, to consider that the thought of a better way might be true. If we can find the courage to hold on to that thought, we might tentatively step out of that dark room and look around at the expanse of beautiful possibilities stretching before us, beautiful but unknown.

We might look back over our shoulder at the room we have just left. It is familiar and perhaps less scary than stepping forward into a place we think we do not know because we have forgotten that it is home. Most of us will retreat into our patterns in the old room several times, many times, countless times, before we are ready, really ready, to explore that better way. We will know that we are ready when the fear of the unknown is less painful than going back into our habitual delusion, when the song of home gives us the courage to be free.

And then, my friend, miracles happen. My own life is proof of that.

It all starts with that thought: There must be a better way.

> *There is absolutely nothing you can create that is not*
> *the expression of your longing to awaken.*
> *~The Jeshua Letters*

The Better Way Is Simple

> *Your soul's deep yearning*
> *Your heart's desire*
> *Is already yours*
> *Now and always*
> *Just let go of everything that is not it*
> *And you will see*

We might think that the "better way" involves complicated lessons or concepts difficult to understand. Not so. Yet it can sometimes appear more complex than it really is. I was once reading a book by a teacher of Daoist healing practices. The book was thick, full of explanations I couldn't understand. Over the years, I had tried to read it several times, only to get bogged down somewhere in the middle and quit.

I understood the author's dilemma. How can words describe the indescribable? More words, different words, cannot explain what the thinking mind cannot label or categorize. So how do we talk about this mystery? Even the author of the *Dao De Jing* acknowledged the issue:

> *My words are very easy to understand*
> *And very easy to practice*
> *Still, no one in the world*
> *Can understand or practice them*

So why try? Because when we glimpse the beauty of that deep mystery, when we pierce the veil of the infinite even for a moment, when the miracle of a single breath astounds us, the strings of our soul are set to humming, and we seek to share this music in harmony with each other in a cosmic jam session. I admit that the efforts to share often obscure as much as they reveal. That is perhaps the nature of the endeavor. We complicate with our words what is, in direct experience, simple, so very simple.

The last time I gave up trying to slog through the book on Daoist healing practices, I called my Daoist teacher in frustration. After I explained why I was calling, here is the rest of our conversation:

Me: Does it really have to be so complicated?

Him: No.

Me: Can we talk more about this?

Him: No need to. The answer is no.

Yet here I am, still talking about it! Imperfect as it is, there is delight in the trying, even though we recognize that our attempts to capture what will remain ever elusive and free will fail.

As Adyashanti says, our goal is to "fail well."

It's all good.

Life becomes extraordinary in its simplicity—the
response to everything that comes to us is the same:
acceptance, compassion, and unconditional love.
~Maharishi Sadasiva Isham

Waking up at Home

All prayers are the same prayer
"I want to go home"
All prayers receive the same answer
"You never left"

The better way for which we search is the one that takes us home. The best thing about the better way is that it will not ever fail. We will all reach our destination of awakening, because, as the word "destination" suggests, it is our destiny.

In the meantime, we sometimes pretend that getting there doesn't matter. "I'm a seeker," someone says at a spiritual retreat. "It's all about the journey," someone else says. We struggle to be content with chronic longing because we get so tired of looking for that special place, that place we think is somewhere "out there." Sometimes it seems like we are almost there, and other times we slump in fatigue as we watch our imagined paradise fade into the distant mist. We tell ourselves that we value the never-getting-there by focusing on the journey, on the seeking. The destination becomes irrelevant.

But is it? I don't think so. I want to be a finder, not a seeker. Why would our souls long so achingly for something if it had no value? The problem isn't that we are looking for the wrong thing. It's not that we are looking for it in the wrong place. It's that we are looking for it at all. Our seeking assumes that there is something we don't have, someplace we are not, and that we must do something to have it or to get there. This very assumption is what keeps us from our soul's deepest desire.

We already have what we most want. We already are where we most want to be. In the movie *Finding Nemo*, my favorite character is Dory, the fish with short-term memory problems. We are like Dory. We don't need to do anything or go anywhere. We just need to remember. Think of all the fish, with their eyes popped open and their mouths forming little "O"s, remembering again and again with every watery breath that they are in the ocean. They are home. As are we.

Our seeking happens mainly in our thoughts. When we quiet our thoughts, our awareness wells up in the silence. When we are caught up in our thoughts of lack, of not getting there, of not doing enough or being enough, we can take a deep breath, then another. As the breath quiets, our mind quiets. Then we can listen in the silence to the silence. We can hear the call of deep mystery welcoming us home.

Deep calls to deep. Home is in the deep. Peace is in the deep. Meaning is in the deep. Truth is in the deep. And Love, too. Beneath the roar of our busy, waterfall lives, there is silence. And it calls to the silence in the deep of our souls, in the deep of all our souls.

Thomas Wolfe wrote that you can't go home again. But you can. Indeed, it is the only place we can go because, when we get there, we realize that we never left. We wake up and see that all our wanderings were but a dream. Like Dorothy, we can click our heels together three times and repeat, "There's no place like home." Then add, "And I'm already here."

And the end of all our exploring
Will be to arrive where we started
And know the place for the first time.
~T. S. Eliot

CHAPTER 2

Start with I Don't Know

Fear comes from thinking
That we know how things should be
And if they are not so
It must surely be our failing
Trust comes hard
To those who carry such a burden
We walk this earth but for a moment
What hubris to think that we know anything

A university professor went to visit a famous Zen master. While the master quietly served tea, the professor pontificated about Zen, holding himself forth as an expert on the topic. As he talked, the master filled the professor's cup to the brim, and then kept pouring. The tea spilled onto the table and then to the floor. The master kept pouring. The professor kept talking until he could no longer ignore the tea puddling around his feet. "Stop! It's overfull! No more will go in!" the professor blurted. "You are like this cup," the master replied. "How can I show you Zen unless you first empty your cup?"

Start with "I don't know." Why not just start with
where you'll end up anyway?
~Adyashanti

Emptying Our Cup

> *Go up, she said*
> *Go up to the mountain top*
> *I think not, he replied*
> *Instead he dove deep*
> *Down down deep*
> *Into the messy muck*
> *Down into the mud*
> *Where the lotus roots grow*

"You know nothing, Jon Snow." If you are a *Game of Thrones* fan, you will recognize this line, spoken to Jon Snow repeatedly by the wildling woman he fell in love with, and who died in his arms with those words on her lips.

The Universe often conspires to remind me that like Jon Snow, everything I think I know…I don't. No matter where I turn—to family, to friends old and new, to martial arts, to life in general—I am confronted by my absolute ignorance of, well, everything. You might be amused, for example, to know that this chapter was the most challenging to write. I could not find a way to structure the topic. I tried and tried. Why isn't this working, I asked in frustration. Oh, I finally realized, I'm trying to write from a cup overflowing with what I think I know about "not knowing."

I had to empty my cup. Again. It is disorienting and decidedly uncomfortable. At the same time, it is intriguing, exciting, and occasionally even fun.

It is, spiritually speaking, where the action is. Outside of my comfort zone is, if I'm willing to look, where I see most clearly my habitual patterns, my stories, my insecurities and fear. It's where I'm invited to stop "seeking" and to start "seeing." It's where I'm given the opportunity to experience the raw beauty and fierce grace of reality, to taste the nectar of truth, to be stripped of all my defenses and emerge pure and powerful … if only for a moment.

It sounds sublime, and it is, but it is also messy, like diving beneath the lotus blossom to its roots in the muck. The muck is where the flower grows. And so it is with us. When we embrace all life offers, excluding nothing, seeing the sacred in every moment, no matter what, then our true nature grows rooted in the depths of darkness to bloom brilliant in the light.

So perhaps a good way to start this chapter is to explore all the ways we think we know things.

Your lack of knowing is not ignorance; your unknowingness is your bowing to life with trust.
~Alana Fairchild

Eye of the Beholder

We don't see things as they are, we see them as we are.
~Anaïs Nin

We think we know that our sensory data are reliable. We assume that what our eyes see, for example, is objectively accurate. If someone questions us, we protest, "I saw it with my own eyes!" But as the quote above indicates, what we think our eyes see might not always be true.

I once had a good laugh at myself at the grocery store when I glanced at a sticker on some bananas in the produce section. I thought the sticker said "Fairy Traded Bananas." How whimsical, I smiled, pausing to picture tiny fairy farmers bringing their harvest to market.

After taking a second look and reading the label as it was, "Fairly Traded Bananas," I got to wondering how often my brain misinterprets my visual data. Probably much more often than I realize.

Here is another example. There is a rhododendron bush outside my window where my desk is. I like to look out the window through its green foliage when I'm at my computer. Once, I saw a squirrel perched on one of the branches, grooming itself. It was so cute, washing its adorable face and stroking its fur. It looked so soft and cuddly, bringing back sweet memories of the friendly pet squirrel I had as a child. It sat on my shoulder while I watched TV and made me laugh with its funny antics as it ran about the house. I loved that squirrel.

I was lost in pleasant reverie when I noticed something was a bit off. Where was its fluffy tail? I looked more closely and recoiled in alarm. It wasn't a squirrel at all. It was a rat! Its naked tail was ugly. Its beady little eyes were full of evil threat. It looked filthy and diseased. I immediately started doing a mental scan of my house, hoping there was no way for it to get inside. I wished one of the feral cats in the neighborhood would come to the rescue.

It was the same little creature going about its business, unaware that in one moment I was gazing upon it with pleasure and enjoyment, and in the next moment I was wishing it a swift and violent death. Nothing in reality had changed, but my perception and the emotional reaction to that perception changed dramatically, giving me an entirely different experience.

We all do it to varying degrees. We are a species that lives for the most part in our minds. The question is not whether we can stop our minds from processing sensory data—we would be unable to function otherwise—but rather whether we can catch ourselves as we process and take a step back to consider the accuracy of our perception. Can we observe how our minds work and explore their pathways with curiosity? Try putting a little webcam on your mind and just follow it around for a while. It might be entertaining, and you might be surprised to discover that our brains sometimes make mistakes. That's not good or bad. It's just what brains do as they try to figure everything out. We can observe the process without judgment and consider what it reveals as we see things "as we are."

> *Come with me, leave your yesterday*
> *your yesterday behind*
> *And take a giant step outside your mind*
> ~Taj Mahal

Weaving Our Memory Tapestry

> *Are you certain this is so*
> *It isn't*
> *Are you certain this is not so*
> *It is*
> *It is neither so*
> *Nor not so*
> *It simply is*
> *...And isn't*

We store our sensory perceptions along with associated judgments and emotions, and over time we add some narrative. These become our memories. Like our sensory perceptions, we think our memories are accurate. Yet we've all watched enough TV and movie crime stories to know that eyewitness testimony is notoriously unreliable, and often becomes even less reliable with the passage of time.

Nothing reveals this unreliability better than the 1950 Japanese film *Rashomon*, the story of a murder told from the perspectives of four witnesses, each of whom tells a very different tale. As you watch the movie, you are caught up in each version, thinking "Oh, this is what really happened." But then a new witness begins to speak, and you are thrown back into the anxiety and frustration of uncertainty.

This film was the origin for the term "Rashomon effect," used to describe the subjective nature of perception. My grandson is enthralled with the technology of virtual reality, but in fact, most of us live our lives in our own, self-created virtual reality. We create this reality not only with our perceptions from sensory data, but also with the stories we tell ourselves about our perceptions, stories that evolve over time until the tether to the original event becomes stretched and thin.

We begin to create these memories at the moment of the triggering event. When something happens, we immediately start telling ourselves a story about it. If what happened was confusing in some way, our stories seek to make sense of it so that we can find comfort in "knowing" what happened. The story often judges what happened as good or bad. Our stories generate feelings of desire or aversion, and are the basis of how we react to what happened. These stories become our reality bubble, within which we experience our lives.

Next time I am in a conversation with someone about what "really happened," I might pause and think about my version and where it came from. What perceptions form the basis of my version? Can I find the "lens" through which those perceptions traveled? Can I let go of the need to be right long enough to explore with open curiosity the stories that I am telling and my attachment to them? I might be surprised to discover the Rashomon effect in my own memory banks.

Truth is a pathless land.
~Krishnamurti

Living Fiction

You are the author of your own life story.
~Susan C. Young

We don't tell ourselves stories only about events. Our favorite subject of storytelling, and the one we are most sure about, is often ourselves. Someone once asked me if I write fiction. No, I replied, I don't write fiction. I live it.

We all do. We tell ourselves stories about our lives and then we believe them. Our emotions are rooted in the narrative. We react and make choices, live and love, fear and hate, enter relationships and leave them, all based on what we have told ourselves about what has happened to us along the way. As a result, I have carried on entire relationships, hidden in embarrassment, been the hero of many stories and the victim of others, suffered hurt feelings, lashed out in anger over perceived wrongs, come to the rescue of people who, now that I think of it, might not have needed any help, and lived numerous versions of my childhood.

We rewrite history many times over, to punish ourselves for what we regret, to reward ourselves for good deeds that grow more grand in the retelling, to hide our shame. Naturally, I prefer the stories that make me look good: the hero rather than the victim, the sage rather than the fool. I like the ones that make me feel transcendently serene rather than agitated and embarrassed.

Sometimes, things happen that defy my attempts to explain and understand and remember what "really" took place. Various stories swirl through my mind. Before one can really settle in, another one replaces it. I can't seem to "catch" one and hold on to it. It's like trying to catch with your hand one slippery fish in a swirling school of hundreds. It leaves me standing in the middle of the maelstrom as a befuddled witness, trying to pick out the "right" story.

So many stories, and we believe them to be true. My sister and I used to joke that our mother could have passed a lie detector test on some of the whoppers she told. She was her own most gullible audience. We all are. I was corrected once in telling a story as my own that had in fact happened to someone else. Over the years, as I told and retold the story of what had happened to my friend, it merged with my own timeline and morphed into a memory of my own life.

Our most cherished tale is of course the most fundamental one—about our own identity. Think of the instructions on forms that give us a list of answers and tell us to check all that apply. All those checked answers put us neatly into boxes. I've noticed that these forms have expanded over the decades to include more choices, but still we are asked to conform ourselves to whatever categories are recognized at the time.

How do you introduce yourself to someone new? What are the first things you want someone to know about you? How have those first things changed over the years? Or how are they different for different audiences? We might find that these introductions represent several images: the one I present to the world, the one I wish to be, the one I fear I really am.

We were once asked in a spiritual direction group to "tell our story" and to listen with an open heart to others tell theirs. The stories were revealing and tender. But still … stories. The deeper question is who we are when we drop all our stories. Try it. Who am I? See every answer as the story it is. Go deeper still. Who am I? Until finally, you inevitably arrive at the only possible answer: I don't know.

If you can be absolutely comfortable with not knowing
who you are, then what's left is who you are—the Being
behind the human, a field of pure potentiality rather
than something that is already defined.
~Eckhart Tolle

"A Girl Has No Name"

I want to understand
To understand what

What is the meaning of this suffering
Suffering has no meaning here. It does not exist

Where is here
Home

I want to come home
You never left

Then why does it seem so far away
Because you have hidden yourself from love

How do I find love
You can't find love because you are love

Please explain
To explain is to separate. Love cannot be explained

Then why are we talking
Who is talking

The most fundamental way that we identify ourselves is simply with our name. The heading of this section is a reference to Arya Stark, a character in *Game of Thrones*, who underwent an initiation that required the complete obliteration of ego. "A girl has no name" was her repeated response to questions about her individual identity, showing that she was no longer attached to her separate self.

The fourth chapter of the *Dao De Jing* uses several images to describe the mysterious and indescribable Dao, or Way. The first image is based on the character 沖, which can be translated as emptiness, as in an empty vessel.

The character itself can be broken into two parts. The left side, which looks like three small lines, means water. The right side, consisting of a horizontal rectangle bisected by a vertical line, means center. So within this "emptiness" character, there is a sense of fluidity as a central quality.

The passage in which the character appears may be translated as "Dao is an empty vessel that is used but never filled." The emptiness of Dao is not a barren wasteland, but on the contrary is a rich source of infinite possibility. I'm reminded again of the Zen master's advice to empty our overflowing cup to make room for enlightenment.

I may not be ready to give up my name, but I do appreciate the concept of releasing my attachment to who I think I am, to who I think I should be. I like the idea of holding my identity lightly, softly, fluidly.

Naming Becomes Reality

Just as we identify ourselves by our name, we identify other things by name and then think we know what they are. We can start to observe the effect on our perceptions of having a name for something, and also how much our brains like to name things.

For example, I was sitting by the creek one spring day watching the light play on the dancing water. When I looked downstream, there was a beautiful cluster of snow-white flowers blooming on a tall stalk leaning out over the creek. As I got closer I could see that the cluster was made up of tiny starburst blossoms.

In that first moment of sight, I experienced a sense of wonder and delight, a gift of exquisite loveliness right there, offering beauty to the trees, the water, the birds and insects…and me. I felt humbly blessed.

All that took place in the nanosecond gap before my thoughts kicked in. My first thought was "What is this flower?" What I meant was the flower's name, its label. I didn't know. Not knowing gave me a subtle feeling of unease as my mind searched for what it might be. I made a plan to take a photo and circulate it to see if someone could tell me. As I got caught up in my thoughts and plans, the initial experience of enchantment quietly faded. It was almost as if the flower no longer existed if I couldn't discover its name.

When I realized what was happening, I was amazed by the rapidity of my shift from a receptive state of appreciation for the flower's beauty to a restless state of thinking. It happened so fast I barely noticed it. But I did notice it, and I felt the loss of that moment of pure enjoyment.

Not only do our brains like to name things but they often don't perceive things that don't have a name. Our brains create our perceived reality from what is named. In a different example, I was walking with a friend in a meadow near her house when she pointed out a wildflower and called it by name. I was enchanted by the name and the sweet little flower. A few weeks later I was walking in the forest at my cabin and saw clusters of these flowers all along the road. I realized that I had walked along this road for years never even noticing this sweet little flower. But once I had a name for it, it became "real" and I saw it all the time. It was like that flower did not exist for me and my eyes did not see it until it had a name.

Names are not bad. They allow us to function in the world and communicate with each other. But the name is not the thing itself. We can miss an opportunity for direct experience and engagement when we mentally insist on a name in order to enjoy something or even to see it in the first place. We miss the miracle.

The name that can be named is not the eternal name.
The nameless is the origin of heaven and earth. The
named is the mother of ten thousand things.
~Dao De Jing

Questioning Assumptions

Some of what we think we know is based on assumptions we make. Many of these assumptions are below our conscious thought, and they direct our thoughts from off stage, so to speak.

Years ago, when I was still new to blogging, a commenter mentioned that he was headed off to bed. Since I was enjoying my morning cup of tea, that caught my attention. Here is the exchange that followed:

Me: Oh, are you a night owl?

Him: No, I'm in Singapore.

Me: Are you traveling or working there?

Him: No, I'm Singaporean Chinese.

Me: I'm studying Chinese.

Him: I don't really speak Chinese.

Me: Wow, you are a one-person lesson in assumptions. Here are the ones I've already made about you: 1) All my readers are in the US so you must be too. 2) If you are not in the US, you must still be an American. 3) If you are ethnic Chinese, you must speak Chinese. Please accept my apology. I really am sorry and thank you for this lesson.

Understand that I am a person who has lived and worked and traveled overseas, including Asia, and I have many friends who are not American. Furthermore, I have a Chinese daughter who doesn't speak Chinese. And yet, I still jumped to these assumptions.

Well, you might say, those are harmless. Indeed, this

commenter and I laughed it off and became close blog friends. But are they harmless? How do my unquestioned assumptions color the way I think about people, about how they act and think, about how they might be safe or not safe, a friend or an enemy?

We go through so much of our daily lives making these snap judgments, and then acting on them without ever questioning them. On a recent run to the grocery store, I decided to see if I could catch all the assumptions I was making. That was sobering. I made assumptions based on how people drove, what they drove, how they parked, what they wore, their ethnicity, their gender, their age, what they had in their shopping carts, with whom they were shopping, how they behaved when we passed in the aisles, how they behaved in the checkout line, and on and on. I'm sure that for every assumption I caught, countless others slipped past me unnoticed.

I don't think we can avoid all assumptions, and I'm not suggesting that we should. This is what our brains are wired to do—identify and categorize. And that serves a purpose. But when we do it so unconsciously, our assumptions can lead to beliefs and actions that might be based on a faulty initial premise.

As the saying goes, don't believe everything you think. If we are willing to take an honest look and become aware of the judgments we automatically make, we might be able to soften our attachment to our own view of things and be wondrously surprised.

> *Your assumptions are your windows on the world.*
> *Scrub them off every once in a while,*
> *or the light won't come in.*
> ~Alan Alda

Reading Our Content Labels

As our brains name and categorize things, and make assumptions about them, we sometimes add a label. That label can carry a judgment. As we become more familiar with our minds and their machinations, we can notice the effects of how we label things.

Years ago, people started reading content labels on their food, discovering things in their food they didn't know were there. Over time, regulations required more disclosure on labels, and people became more knowledgeable about understanding the significance of various ingredients.

That got me thinking about how we use labels in general. We use them to identify or categorize something, like species or brand names. Labels are intrinsic to communication and information, and serve a useful purpose.

Labels can also affect our experience through implied judgment. In a conversation with a friend about his child, for example, he described a particular situation as a "problem" and was feeling very worried and frustrated. When I asked him why he thought the situation was a "problem," he described an outcome that he considered "bad." This led to an exploration of the effect of labeling the situation as a problem and labeling the anticipated outcome as bad. When he was able to think beyond the negative judgments, he was able to look at the situation with a more expansive view. He visibly calmed down and viewed the scenario in a more neutral way.

In another conversation, a friend was relating an encounter that left him very upset. A person had objected to something my friend said. My friend tried to explain, making matters worse. The other person threw out a label. My friend denied it.

As I was listening, I could understand why the other person might have taken offense at my friend's initial comment, which could have been understood several different ways. But any effort to have meaningful dialogue was quickly obliterated by the labeling, which became the focus of the escalating argument.

I'm not taking sides here on whether the label was justified. The point is that any opportunity for my friend to understand how his initial comment might have been experienced by the listener was lost in the debate about the label. Correct or not, the label ended any genuine communication. And the continued defensiveness against the label hindered any honest reflection about hidden assumptions or biases my friend's initial comment might have revealed.

So labels can be useful, but they can also be obstacles, especially when unquestioned, as in the first conversation, or when used as an attack or defense, as in the second.

These conversations have made me take a closer look at some of the labels I use and how they affect my assessment of a situation, my emotional reactions, and my ability to have meaningful communication. I'm going to make more effort to "read" the content of labels I use and see what the hidden ingredients are!

> *Once you label me, you negate me.*
> ~Søren Kierkegaard

The Trap of Belief

> *Your belief does not make Truth true*
> *Truth is ever true and can be nothing else*
> *All else is false*
> *And cannot be made true by thought*
> *So believe or do not believe*
> *It does not matter*

In questioning what we think we know, one of the most challenging areas to explore is our beliefs. Our minds love beliefs because, as we've discussed, our minds are designed to seek certainty. Studies show that we are more afraid of uncertainty than we are of actual physical pain. That is just the way our brains are wired. We've all experienced this. Maybe we have rushed to a decision because the stress of waiting for more information or for the clarity of inner guidance was intolerable. Maybe we were quick to believe something about someone instead of pausing to consider that our assumptions might be mistaken.

One time I heard a random sound that my brain couldn't immediately identify, so my brain told me I heard a dog barking. In the next moment, my brain recalculated and told me that the sound I heard was a train whistle in the distance. It didn't sound anything at all like a dog barking. When the sound first vibrated in my ear, my brain couldn't wait one extra nanosecond to identify the sound correctly, so it just picked something random rather than wait in uncertainty. What's more, there was a transitory sense of confusion and anxiety as my brain took in more information and changed its conclusion. It was like my brain, having decided incorrectly, was loath to endure any hint of doubt and give up the mistake.

In the big scheme of life, whether the sound I heard was a barking dog or a train whistle isn't important. But consider the significance of my brain's desperate grab for an immediate answer, any answer, and its reluctance to give that answer up in the face of contrary evidence. Consider that significance in the context of things that really matter. Beliefs divide families and nations, bind groups together and exclude others. People will kill for their beliefs. And die for them.

Beliefs are powerful because we are so attached to them and identified with them. Some beliefs are so fundamental to our sense of well-being that the slightest hint of changing or releasing them threatens annihilation. No wonder we are such an anxious and fearful species. We have based our very existence on the thoughts and stories that our minds come up with and then latch onto.

When hunters in Africa want to catch a monkey, they carve a small hole in something stationary, like a tree trunk or a gourd secured with a rope. They put food in the hole, stand back, and wait. The monkey will reach into the hole and grab a handful, but with a fist full of food the monkey can't get its hand back out. Even as the hunter approaches, the monkey will frantically pull and scream, but it won't let go. It is caught.

All the monkey has to do is let go. If it releases what it grasps so tightly in its fist, it will be free. Like that monkey, sometimes I find myself trapped by my own attachment to a belief or judgment or desire or emotion. Perhaps I am holding onto resentment over something that happened years ago. Or I am judging a person or a situation in a way that isolates me or causes me fear.

We sometimes admire someone for the strength of their convictions. But the word "conviction" can mean being declared guilty of a crime, as well as a firmly held belief. Do my firmly held beliefs in some way imprison me?

What would it take to open my hand, unlike that trapped monkey, and be free? It's not necessary to pry my fingers off by force. If I can explore the nature of the belief and its importance to me with curiosity, maybe I will feel my grip loosen. Maybe not, in which case I can explore with compassion that unwillingness to let go and trust that I will let go when I'm ready.

Some of us equate beliefs with faith, but they are not the same. Beliefs are static. We become attached to and identified with our beliefs. Beliefs don't allow dissent. They lock us in just like those trapped monkeys. Faith, on the other hand, at least the way I think about it, is a dynamic relationship of trust, whether that is trust in God, the Universe, or our own inner wisdom. Faith does not require belief. Indeed, as Adyashanti says, "belief is an absolute and utter lack of faith." Sit with that for a moment.

It makes sense if we go back to what we know about our brains. Belief satisfies our mind's need to know. Belief is safe because it gives us the security of certainty. But there is no peace, because on some level we fear that we have chosen wrongly, and thus we seek constant confirmation, and defend our beliefs with insistence and even anger or violence. Belief needs to be right.

Faith doesn't need to be right. Right and wrong are meaningless to faith. Faith asks us to trust rather than to know. Our brains don't like this. But our souls rejoice, as faith invites us into the sacred dance of the present moment, singing the music of creation, embracing us with infinite awareness. Then, and only then, do we experience the peace that passes all understanding.

Thoughts take us into illusion. Beliefs imprison us there. ... You have abandoned truth for belief.
~Leonard Jacobson

The Pink T-Shirt

That last section might have been a lot to take in, so here is something a little more light-hearted to consider.

When my daughter was a child, she would put a pink T-shirt on her head and pretend it was long hair. She would stand in front of the mirror swishing it around and styling it. Yes, that girl could braid a T-shirt and make it into a ponytail or a bun.

One day we were getting ready to go to the store. She ran to get the pink T-shirt and when it was arranged to her liking, she headed to the door.

Looking back at me, she asked, "Will people think I have long hair?"

"No, sweetie," I said gently, "they will think you have a pink T-shirt on your head."

She paused as a shadow of doubt flitted across her brow. But just for a moment.

"No they won't," she said resolutely as she flipped her long, cottony tresses over her shoulder and skipped away.

That is one of my favorite stories of her irrepressible childhood. I was reminded of it recently when I caught myself in a pink hair story about a situation that I wanted to be a certain way. I told myself that the situation was indeed how I imagined it to be, and was puzzled and frustrated by all the evidence right in front of me that didn't comport with my preferred narrative.

It didn't work, of course. I saw pretty quickly what I was doing, and still I was reluctant to let my dream go. The hold that our delusions have on us is strong. And so I did what I've learned to do when out of sync with what is. I began to inquire. What is the nature of this illusion? Of the reluctance to let it go? Where do I feel it in my body? What is underneath it?

I became aware of the energy it took to sustain the illusion, and I could already feel how tiring it was. I could observe the suffering of attachment, even a minor attachment such as this one. I saw, as is often the case, that our attachments are rarely about the object or story of our desire. We have to go deep for the source to be revealed. And as my hold softened, compassion welled up to soothe the loss of the illusion I had held so dear.

Another term for pretend is make-believe, but perhaps there is a difference. If I'm pretending, I know I am. It's fun to explore the vast terrain of imagination. But when I "make" myself "believe" what I'm pretending, I create a dissonance between what is and what I'm wanting it to be.

I pulled off the pink T-shirt with gratitude and lovingly put it away.

> *It is far better to grasp the universe as it really is than*
> *to persist in delusion, however satisfying*
> *and reassuring.*
> ~Carl Sagan

Releasing Something Every Day

> *When engaged with learning,*
> *every day something is acquired*
> *When engaged with Dao,*
> *every day something is released*
> ~Dao De Jing

Now, after exploring all the ways we think we know things, let's explore the wisdom of not knowing.

Learning in our everyday lives is a process of acquiring knowledge, information, skill. There is nothing wrong with that. "Learning" in our spiritual lives, however, is a process of "unlearning," letting go of whatever it is that blocks our awareness of and engagement with the present moment. We enter what an anonymous Christian mystic in the 14th century called "the cloud of unknowing." Here, he wrote, is where we meet God.

It's not always easy. As we've seen, we can be very attached to the very things that hinder our awakened union with the divine, such as judgments, opinions, beliefs, and stories.

For me, I can look back at how desperately I latched onto various identities, and how loath I was to give them up. When I have gone through major life transitions, one of the hardest things has been giving up who I thought I was in whatever stage I was transitioning out of. This was especially true in my younger years.

Okay, if I'm not going to be a back-to-the-land hippie, I'll be a pianist. That didn't work out, so I'll be a lawyer. That worked out for many years, and along the way I added some other identities. I'm a mother, a teacher, a martial artist, a blogger, a grandmother, and more. Each one has a story. As I've gotten older, some stories have changed or dropped away. It's not as traumatic as before because my attachment is not as deep-rooted or desperate.

In addition to the external identities, I have had inner ones as well. I am a good person, an ethical person, an intelligent person, a spiritual person, a person who sometimes has mystical experiences. And of course there are the shadow identities, the ones I would prefer to keep hidden. I am sometimes a person who is judgmental, impatient, fearful, petty. These various identities have stories too. All my identities, external and internal, favored and unfavored, are all just stories.

Several years ago, I engaged in what I called an apprenticeship with grief. As part of that process, I used on occasion a non-dominant-hand writing method that accesses a deeper, more intuitive voice, for lack of a better description. Using this method I had an ongoing dialogue with grief, who was a wise and gentle teacher. At one point, I was expressing frustration over not having a clear idea of what exactly I was grieving.

Grief answered, "You are grieving the end of thinking, of thinking that you know who you are."

We all function in the world in various roles. It can't be otherwise. But we can wear our roles loosely, like comfortable clothes, without mistaking them for the essence of who we are. We can practice, as the quote says, letting go of something every day.

> *Some of us think holding on makes us strong; but*
> *sometimes it is letting go.*
> ~Hermann Hesse

The Freedom of Not Knowing

I was never a legit Trekkie but I did enjoy and was inspired by two of the series: *Next Generation* and *Voyager*.

Each of those series had a crew member characterized by intellectual and logical prowess: Data, the android in *Next Generation*, and Tuvok, the Vulcan in *Voyager*. Occasionally they were confronted with a question they could not answer.

"What is the composition of the gasses in that nebula?"

"What is the origin of that ship speeding towards us on an intercept course?"

"What dimension did these aliens just emerge from?"

When unable to answer, Data or Tuvok would simply reply "unknown."

When feeling that urge to understand what cannot be understood, to describe what cannot be described, to have certainty where none exists, I sometimes interrupt my endless mind loops with a simple word—unknown.

It's a relief to admit that I don't know, even though the mind hates that. My mind is useful for many things, and I appreciate its contribution to my life. Confronted with mystery, however, our minds continue to search for an answer, like a phone out of range roaming for a signal. That's fine if the mystery is about what is making that scratching sound in the attic, but it doesn't work when the question is beyond the limits of mind, when the answer is not only unknown, but unknowable.

Not one to give up, the mind solves the dilemma by latching onto an answer. Then a problem arises when someone else's mind latches onto a different answer. Which answer is The Answer? How can we know? We can't. We cannot think our way to truth. Thinking is always one step away from truth. Truth just is, regardless of what we think or don't think. When we drop everything we think we know, there it is, shining like a light that has been uncovered, shining as it always has and always will.

But as soon as we try to think about it, or understand it, or explain it, it disappears again, not because it isn't there but because our efforts to hold it in our minds block our inner sight. As *The Sound of Music* song asks, how do you hold a moonbeam in your hand?

Someone once joked that I'm like Oprah. (Really, they were joking.) Oh no, I replied. Oprah's monthly magazine ends with a column titled "What I Know for Sure." Oprah knows something for sure at least twelve times a year. I don't know anything…ever.

This was brought home to me when I had tea with a friend who spent our whole time together explaining her evolving theories of awakening. While much of what she said was fascinating and thought provoking, there were times when I couldn't keep up with the pace of her excited revelations, and I confess my brain drifted in and out of attention to her words. Instead, I became intrigued by the global structure of her analysis, and by her certainty that she had things figured out.

On the way home, as I was contemplating my friend's grasp of the knowledge that she seemed so sure of, I looked down at what I was wearing and laughed out loud. The Chinese characters on my T-shirt meant "I really don't know."

It's okay not to know. My law students often expressed appreciation for my willingness to admit when I didn't know something. They said I would get excited and invite everyone to figure it out together. Those were some of the best classes because we were all engaged with each other in dynamic inquiry.

Not knowing. It's the place, and perhaps the only place, where authentic connection happens, because when we are in that place of not knowing, we are an open rather than a closed system. It's where our cup is empty and has space for something else.

In the beginner's mind there are many possibilities,
but in the expert's mind there are few.
~Shunryu Suzuki

Living with Beginner's Mind in an Expert World

Footprints lead to the shore of the sea
Beyond that point no trace remains
~Rumi

Even if we embrace the freedom of not knowing, there are times when we still like to be a know-it-all. For example, after practicing tai chi for many years, I started a class at a different martial arts school. Although not new to tai chi, I was new to this school, so I was sort of a beginner and not a beginner at the same time. Some things were familiar to me, but every school, and even every teacher, has their own way of doing things, so there is always a steep learning curve at the outset.

The students began class all together doing warm-up exercises and then broke into small groups according to their level. Based on my prior experience, I thought I was moving through the preliminary stuff quickly, and I was eager to get to the more advanced material. But after several classes, the teacher placed me in a beginner group with people who had not done any tai chi at all, ever. The instruction was at the most basic introductory level.

It didn't take me long to start feeling impatient, chafing at the slow pace, wishing to be in the group that was working on material more suited to my level, at least in my not-so-humble opinion. I felt frustrated that the teacher couldn't immediately see that a mistake had been made and move me to the other group.

When I caught myself, I wondered what in the heck was going on with me. My ego knickers were in a knot. I was violating every basic principle of tai chi and everything I've learned from the *Dao De Jing*. I was not being present. I was distracted and judgmental. I was wanting reality to be different and trying to make it conform to my desire. I was being disrespectful (at least in my thoughts) to the teacher. I was caught up in my mind's narrative and missing the opportunity to practice in the situation I was in, which is really the only practice there is.

One of the slogans I've trained with for years is "Don't insist. Don't resist." I was doing both, unlike my fellow students in the beginning group who were fully engaged with what was happening. So apparently the beginning group was right where I belonged. I clearly had a lot to learn. Humility goes hand in hand with beginner's mind. As I said to a friend after recounting my story about class, I might not learn a lot about tai chi in this class, but I'm going to learn a lot about myself! And perhaps that is the same thing after all.

Life is a long lesson in humility.
~James M. Barrie

It's Still Okay to Know What You Know

One of the images often used to describe Dao, or a person who is aligned with Dao, is the Chinese character 朴. It means simple, pure, in the original or basic state. It literally means an uncarved block of wood. In that uncarved block are many possible forms that might emerge under the carver's hands. This is the infinite, undifferentiated potential of Dao, which manifests into the myriad forms of the created universe. To me, it also represents the concept of beginner's mind. It suggests an attitude of openness, curiosity, lack of prejudgment, a willingness to learn, to engage with what is, as it is, in the present moment.

As we mature, we make choices that set us on a certain path. We might have a career, settle down with a partner, raise children. Or not. As we age, we realize that certain choices are no longer open to us. Just as carving a block of wood reveals one form as it eliminates others, we develop skills and expertise in some areas of life while letting go of other paths.

So what does it mean to have beginner's mind in the midst of life's commitments and limitations and choices? Someone remarked to me that he didn't want to start over all the time, if that is what beginner's mind required, abandoning the skills that his career and life experience brought him. I empathized. As we become experts in certain areas, how do we maintain a freshness and wonder in the newness of each day, each moment?

To me, the focus of beginner's mind is internal rather than external. After all, the term is beginner's "mind," not beginner's "life." It doesn't mean ignoring the wisdom and knowledge we have gained, but it does encourage us to apply this wisdom and knowledge with a fresh perspective. It means pausing sometimes to view a situation without thinking that we know how things should be, to consider that we might not know what the best outcome is, to admit that we don't know everything we think we do.

Above all, beginner's mind is based in trust. When confronted with a challenge that upsets or worries me, sometimes my initial instinct is to get in there and "fix" it, but if I can step back and settle down into beginner's mind, I can listen and watch. I can trust that the way forward will become apparent, like a form that emerges from the uncarved block of wood, or like murky water that clears when it is allowed to settle.

What I've learned most of all from living in beginner's mind is that the way forward will always be one of love.

I would love to live like a river flows, carried by the surprise of its own unfolding.
~John O'Donohue

The Universe Will Always Help You Out

Trust life to remind you frequently that you will end up with not knowing. For example, when I'm sparring with my martial arts teacher and somehow manage to get him in a hold, he will pause and look at me.

"Oh, you got me."

A moment later, just as I'm feeling smug, he simply melts away like smoke and I'm left holding nothing. Then he says with a twinkle,

"Do you?"

Life is often like that. It's a series of revelations that whatever I think I know or understand, I don't. I thought I understood a situation. I didn't. I thought I was being helpful. I wasn't. I thought I had a particular relationship with someone. I didn't. I believed something to be true. It wasn't.

It felt like the Universe was taunting me, when really it was teaching me.

Oh, you got this…. Do you?

Over a period of a couple of years I experienced a pattern of revelation. Each revelation allowed me to release something I held on to, not always gracefully or gratefully, I admit. Each one went deeper, layer beneath layer. Then the big one, the one I had held on to my whole life. When I finally released that one too, I thought, "Whew, it all led up to this. I've released it all. I'm done. That was the grand finale of releasing."

Was it?

The process continued and brought yet another deeply held belief into question. Really? I have to release even that?

Even that.

Then what's left? Oh, I get it.

Or do I?

How have I been so blessed
To have this life
To be life
Released from all knowing
Falling gratefully
Into the current of the infinite

CHAPTER 3

Willingness To Trust

Trust
Like the trees
In patient being
Resting in acceptance
Of whatever comes
The perfect surrender
Of majestic trees
Quietly showing us
How it's done

Emptying our cups and embracing beginner's mind requires trust. We can buy a one-way ticket to Kathmandu and meditate at the feet of masters…and none of it will matter if we don't trust our own inner process of remembering who we are and listening to the guidance of our innate inner wisdom. It's like that team building exercise when one person closes their eyes and falls backwards, trusting their team members to catch them. Awakening is the great trust fall of life. And this is life's promise to you: "I will catch you every time without fail, because you have never, ever, not even for one moment, been separated from my embrace."

Inner peace doesn't come with understanding.
It comes with trusting.
~Rumi

Trust Where You Are

A martial arts buddy shared that his teacher reminds him from time to time to "trust where you are." He explained that when he does not trust where he is in his body, it is easy to move him off balance, because his center is raised up in a way that makes him top heavy, like an inverted triangle wobbling on its point, and his body becomes tense. In contrast, when he relaxes and sinks his center, trusting his alignment to absorb or deflect force, it is difficult to move him. He is then more like a triangle resting on its base.

Like so many things I learn in martial arts, this instruction to trust where you are applies to life in general. We get so much advice about lowering stress, living in joy, not worrying all the time, having a positive attitude, being present, and more. A thread runs through all this advice—trust. So what is it that we are trusting?

Chögyam Trungpa Rinpoche and Bishop Desmond Tutu are among many wisdom teachers who have written about the basic goodness of the universe, and the basic goodness of human nature. The Bible assures us that all things work together for good. The *Dao De Jing* compares Dao to water, moving effortlessly according to its nature. All these sources suggest that there is a natural order to things, which we can trust. This natural order encompasses everything in creation. This "everything" includes us.

We spend a lot of energy trying to determine our best way forward, analyzing pros and cons, gathering data, predicting outcomes of various choices, and second guessing ourselves. When our thoughts spin off like this, our center is raised up in our head, in our thinking mind, disconnected from our foundation. We are top heavy like the inverted triangle, and as a consequence, we live life out of balance, out of alignment with the natural harmony of the universe. We try to force or resist, not trusting where we are.

Conversely, when we trust where we are, we are present with whatever is going on. We are relaxed and confident. We are stable on our foundation. This doesn't mean that we don't ever move to a new location or try something new or seek to improve our skills. It means that no matter where we are or what is going on, we are fully present, attuned to inner guidance, knowing that every moment we are exactly where we need to be, in harmony with the natural unfolding of our lives.

Like the maps in parks, malls, and hotels that have a little arrow pointing to a spot "YOU ARE HERE," we realize that we literally and figuratively can't be anywhere else than exactly where we are. So be there—accept it, embrace it, trust it.

> *As soon as you trust yourself,*
> *you will know how to live.*
> ~Johann Wolfgang von Goethe

Fear Is the Trust Killer

> *I must not fear. Fear is the mind-killer. Fear is the*
> *little-death that brings total obliteration. I will face*
> *my fear. I will permit it to pass over me and through*
> *me. And when it has gone past I will turn the inner*
> *eye to see its path. Where the fear has gone there will*
> *be nothing. Only I will remain.*
> ~Frank Herbert

We can't talk about trust without talking about fear. This litany against fear from the book *Dune* resonated with me when I was young. I memorized it and would recite it when needed, which was often. Now, decades later, it resonates still, perhaps even more so because over the years I have lived its wisdom so many times.

Some say that fear can be a good thing when it warns us of danger. I see their point, but even so, I submit that it isn't fear that enhances our survival, but rather an instinctive assessment of a possible threat. Fear can block the trust we need to listen to our inner wisdom. It is this wisdom that protects us, not fear.

So yes, instincts can warn us of danger and some people would call that helpful fear. But the fear I speak of here is the fear in our minds, in our thoughts. This is the fear that spins out dire scenarios, most of which never happen. This is the fear that hinders our response to the challenging scenarios that inevitably do arise. When we can step away from our fearful thinking, we can better assess our situation, whatever it is, and respond appropriately.

People sometimes ask me if I've ever had to use my martial arts training in a real life self-defense situation. Yes, twice. Both times I was able to deflect the threat and move out of danger, not with my (nonexistent) superior fighting skills, but with words. In reflecting on those two incidents, what strikes me most is how calm I was. Alert, yes, very alert. But unafraid. Staying calm and unafraid allowed me to respond to the threat with an assurance that was reflected in my demeanor and in my tone of voice. And that, more than anything, I think, led to a de-escalation of the danger and kept me safe.

Sometimes we don't even realize we're afraid. Fear wears many masks: for example, anger, hatred, anxiety, judgment. We don't always see fear behind these masks. When I'm afraid, I feel weak or helpless. In contrast, when I'm angry, I feel strong, which is why anger is such a powerful emotion. But underneath the anger, there is always fear. We won't overcome the rage unless we address the fear.

Fear can also look like fearlessness. Years ago, a friend observed that the driving force in my life was fear. At the time, I saw myself as a bold person, taking daring risks, living adventures all over the world. I dismissed what my friend said, thinking that she must not know me very well, and probably was not such a good friend after all. Time proved that, on the contrary, she knew me better than most, and certainly better than I knew myself. Only by acknowledging the undertow of quiet terror that nipped at my heels and kept me on the move was I able to do the work necessary to release its hold on me.

The release of fear can take practice. A therapist once suggested using the simple phrase "I am safe" when my mind is caught in fear's snare. We can also try a reality check. When one of my grandchildren is afraid, I ask them to look around the room to see if in fact there is anything that resembles whatever monsters are haunting their thoughts. Once we've established that the fear is in their thinking, I help them find something else for their minds to do. We read a book, tell a story, whatever it takes to shift the focus.

We can do the same. Rather than tell ourselves not to be afraid, which just calls attention to the fear and gives it more power, we can catch our mind's attention and draw it away from fearful thoughts. Then, rather than judging, rejecting, or criticizing ourselves for having fearful thoughts, we can begin to explore the illusory nature of fear with curiosity and compassion.

The opposite of love is fear, but what is all encompassing can have no opposite.
~A Course in Miracles

Making Peace with Fear

Beyond the momentary respite of a phrase like "I am safe," or a reality check of our surroundings, how do we release fear's grip on our minds? What I appreciate about *Dune's* litany against fear is the recognition that if not resisted or denied, fear will dissipate on its own. Not by struggle, but by being inwardly still, we empty ourselves of resistance, thus allowing space for the fear to move over or through us. Sounds easy but we all know it isn't.

The Buddhist teacher Pema Chödrön tells the story of a young warrior sent out to battle fear. The young warrior balked, but her teacher insisted. On the appointed day, the young warrior stepped onto the field of battle, feeling small and unprepared. Fear stood on the other side, huge and fierce. Her knees shaking, the young warrior bowed respectfully and asked fear, "How do I defeat you?" Fear, surprised by her gesture, thanked her for showing respect and replied, "My weapons are that I talk fast and get in your face. Then you get completely unnerved, and you do whatever I say. If you don't do what I say, I have no power."

I love this story, and it has guided me through many encounters with fear. I am grateful to fear for revealing to me the key to its own defeat. However, no matter how many times fear's instruction to resist its demands has proven effective, it remains a challenge to follow it. This is partly because we don't always recognize fear's voice.

The story portrays fear the way most of us think of it—like a big, scary, screaming monster. But I've found that fear can also look less threatening, even alluring. Not yelling but whispering, even sounding very reasonable.

So how do we know if fear is speaking to us? We know because fear always tells us to separate, to close our hearts, to be ever vigilant and on guard. Fear tells us we are powerless and alone. Fear urges us to try to control what we can't control, thus affirming that our efforts are futile, and reinforcing our feeling of helplessness. This is often experienced as an urge to interfere, sometimes disguised as well-meaning intentions. My own little reminder in this regard is that if you say "interfere" out loud, it sounds just like "enter fear."

Whether fear screams or whispers, we've all felt that urge to do what fear tells us. When we listen to it, we play right into fear's hands. Fear has indeed proven itself the mind-killer by hijacking our thoughts and spinning out stories that we believe.

Fear is often so distressing that we are desperate to escape it. It is this desperation that fear counts on, because we are then willing to follow fear's instructions, thinking it will lead to relief. Southwest Airlines had a great series of commercials in which some hapless individual would be in a horrifyingly embarrassing situation. The voice over would say, "Want to get away? Low fares to...." You knew that poor person would jump on the first plane to anywhere!

But if we can recognize when fear is speaking, we can claim our power, our power to choose. We can choose to do what fear says, or we can choose not to. We can choose to be still, to hold steady in openness and allow fear to move on through.

Sometimes, when I recognize that I'm afraid, I tell myself that the images or stories in my mind are not real. If I can breathe into the discomfort, stay still and present, and wait, then amazingly, I can sense fear's power begin to fade. My thinking clears up, and I recognize that following fear's direction would have led me astray. I often experience compassion soothing my troubled spirit, like a mother soothing a child waking up from a bad dream. And then, as the litany promises, we will see that fear was nothing. It has gone past and we remain.

Living in Trust

*The words are spoken in silence
Heard only in the heart
Do not doubt what they reveal
More real than any heard in mind
Trust what is known beyond knowing
And be not misled by thought
That seeks to paint illusion bright
Be thou thus ignited
With truth that always burns
Deep
Deep*

As we make our peace with fear by recognizing its voice and choosing not to follow it, we can begin to shift our focus to what it means to live in trust. Many of us are raised to believe that we cannot and should not trust our inner guidance. We are taught that we must look outside ourselves to some external authority to be told what is true. As we learn to "trust where we are," to claim the freedom and responsibility for our choices, to listen to our inner wisdom in alignment with the natural harmony of the universe, we may still encounter times of uncertainty.

During one such period in my own life, when I felt like I had lost my inner balance, I entered a time of self-reflection to explore what was blocking my way. I saw myself struggling with various feelings and circumstances, which I then judged and tried to dispel or control. (That never works.) I finally saw that the problem was doubt. I saw that if I didn't trust the natural energy of the universe to flow through me, if I didn't trust my inner voice of wisdom to guide me, if I didn't trust my practice to carry me through challenging times, then it wouldn't matter how much I meditated or aspired or anything else. Doubt would block all the blessings. I didn't need to figure everything out. I didn't need to fix anything. I didn't need to make myself do better or be better. I needed only to stay aligned in the center of what is…and trust.

During this time of self-reflection, three images kept coming to me, speaking to me, each with its own lesson to teach me about trust.

Choosing Trust

The first image was Orpheus, a character from Greek mythology, who went into the underworld to beg for the return of his beloved wife Eurydice, who had died. Hades granted his wish, but with a condition. Eurydice would follow behind Orpheus on the journey out of the underworld. Orpheus was forbidden to look back at her until they both had crossed back into the land of the living.

Orpheus set out, but all along the way he could hear nothing behind him. As he finally approached the exit, he could not stand the uncertainty a moment longer. He turned, only to see Eurydice, who had been behind him the whole way, fade back into the underworld forever.

The underworld is a place of mystery, unknown and unknowable by our thinking minds. Yet this mystery holds what we most long for: union with the Beloved, union from which we all emerged and in which we all live, union that we've never left, but that we've forgotten and seek to remember.

When we enter the mystery of unknowing, we are promised that what we want is ours, has always been ours. But to experience it, we must trust that it is there, for when we doubt, it fades away.

The good news is that, unlike poor Orpheus who was barred from a second attempt to enter the underworld and bring forth his beloved, we are allowed endless opportunities to sink into the sacred embrace. Each time we choose to trust, we learn to trust more deeply and to sustain our trust longer, before our thoughts sow doubt and we forget once again that we are infinitely and unconditionally loved. We repeat the process until we finally step into the land of the living, trusting that the Beloved is with us always, that we are always one with Love, that we are forever blessed.

*Your soul will keep its promise to Itself—the promise
of return. Trust in the peace of that knowing.*
~Emmanuel's Book II

Maintaining Trust

The second image that came to me in connection to living in trust was the Bible story of Peter walking across the water to Jesus. The disciples were in a boat during a storm and saw Jesus walking towards them on the water. Peter wanted to try so Jesus called Peter to come to him. Peter left the boat and walked across the water toward Jesus. As long as his eyes were on Jesus, he walked on the stormy sea without difficulty. But as soon as he looked away and saw the waves whipped up by the wind, he became afraid and began to sink. He called out, and Jesus lifted him up and took him to the safety of the boat.

This image reminds me of the importance of maintaining our focus on abiding in trust. As long as Peter's eyes were locked on Jesus, he was unconcerned about the storm and about the implausibility of being able to walk on water. It was only when his attention faltered with doubt that he lost his alignment and began to sink. Peter might have benefitted by heeding Stephen Covey's advice: "The main thing is to keep the main thing the main thing."

Perhaps some of us can remember a time when we listened to and trusted our inner guidance despite all the logical or practical reasons why we shouldn't. In my own life, amazing things have happened, things I could not have planned or foreseen, when I stepped forward in trust. This has happened enough times that now I listen for the call and follow it in faith (at least most of the time).

I find it reassuring that in Peter's story, disaster did not follow doubt. When Peter began to sink into the stormy sea, Jesus took him to the boat where he was safe. Peter didn't drown; he was simply returned to his normal, rational security. But he missed out on the miracle that was his as long as he walked in trust.

Like Peter, we cut ourselves off from the extraordinary when we ignore our inner wisdom, perhaps because it doesn't make sense, because others tell us it's crazy, or because we can't see where it's leading us. Sometimes we prefer to play it rationally safe and settle for the ordinary. We open our umbrellas over our heads when the Universe is showering us with blessings and guiding us with rainbows.

But when we take a deep breath and choose to trust with unwavering focus, then there is a synchronicity of alignment that allows us to walk on the water of life, undisturbed by the waves, buoyed by sacred mystery, forever loved and free.

Trusting Even When You Can't

The third image that came to me in connection with living in trust was another character from Greek mythology, Odysseus, who knew that on his voyage home after the Trojan War, his ship would have to pass the deadly coast where the Sirens called enchantingly to passing ships. Their song was so irresistible that sailors would go mad with desire and turn their ships toward the shore only to be dashed against the rocks and die.

Odysseus wanted to hear the Sirens without the usual outcome and devised a plan to keep everyone safe and the ship intact. He had his crew plug their ears with wax and lash him tightly to the mast, with instructions to ignore anything he said or did until they were safely past the danger. Predictably, when he heard the Sirens singing, Odysseus was overcome with desire. He screamed and threatened and fought his bonds, but the ropes held fast, and his crew carried on with their duties, oblivious to the temptation and the ranting of their captain.

The connection between this third image and living in trust was less immediately obvious to me than the first two. Understanding came gradually from my experience with Daoist healing arts. Our teacher often reminded us to "trust the practice," especially when we were discouraged. Even when life was not flowing easily but rather tossing me on stormy seas, my practice protected me.

When we practice living in trust long enough, we find that our practice carries us through the tough times. Like Odysseus, we are held fast, not by ropes but by love's sacred embrace, protected and cherished, until we remember once again that it has always been so.

When you pass through the waters, I will be with you;
and when you pass through the rivers, they will not
sweep over you. When you walk through the fire, you
will not be burned.
~Isaiah 43:2

The Labyrinth of Life

Trust in the Lord with all your heart and lean
not on your own understanding. In all your ways
acknowledge Him, and He shall direct your paths.
~Proverbs 3:5-6

I've had many occasions in recent years to ride in the car while one of my daughters is driving. When they get in the car, they automatically program the GPS for their destination and follow the moving arrow along with the spoken directions. The directions lead them one step at a time, guiding them just as far as the next turn. Even when it is somewhere that, at least in my opinion, they should know how to get to, they turn over the directions to the GPS and trust that it will get them there. They are content to know only the immediate instruction, and they seem unperturbed that the rest of the route is a mystery, revealed only as needed. It is, I've come to appreciate, a lesson in trust, like walking a labyrinth.

Unlike a maze, there are no wrong turns in a labyrinth. Yes, there are twists and turns, but the path leads unerringly to the center. You cannot get lost, so you can be confident that the path you are on will take you where you want to go. And yet, how it will get you there is unclear. The winding path defies your efforts visually see the entire course. In fact, taking your eyes off the path to look too far ahead will only confuse you. Your attention needs to be on the path under your feet so you can see where the next step is.

Walking a labyrinth is a meditation in being present, trusting that no matter how many twists and turns you take, you are being led without mistake on the path to God (or the center, or your true being, or enlightenment, or whatever term you want to use). And once you reach the center, after resting in the power of its energy, you turn and walk back out, again trusting the path to lead you, this time back into the world, bringing with you the deep peace of the center.

When we live our life like a labyrinth walk, we trust our inner guidance to lead us. We live in mindful awareness of the present moment, patient until the next moment reveals our way. We release our need to control, our attachment to certainty, our fear of failing. Our inner wisdom will guide us on our path of destiny to an awakened remembrance of who we are, who we've always been. As many times as we forget, the labyrinth path will return us to our center, and from that center we move through our lives, in trust, at peace, with joy.

I don't scoff at my daughters anymore for their reliance on their GPS. It might not be as infallible as the labyrinth, but perhaps it is their version of a practice in being present and trusting in the goodness of the universe.

> *If we learn to love the earth, we will find labyrinths,*
> *gardens, fountains, and precious jewels! A whole new*
> *world will open itself to us. We will discover what it*
> *means to be truly alive.*
> ~Teresa of Ávila

"This Is What I'm Doing"

One aspect of trust is owning the choices you make and taking responsibility for your life.

During a conversation with a martial arts friend and mentor, I shared my sense of where-do-I-go-from-here lack of clear direction in my practice. Did I want a different teacher? Did I want to learn a new form or a new style or a new weapon?

Describing his own shift in practice, my friend explained that he had dropped the notion of a specific teacher or learning a particular style. Instead, he was going back to fundamentals and exploring wherever his curiosity led him, following the guidance of his body's wisdom after years of practice. Striking out on his own, everything felt fresh and exciting again. He said without apology or need to justify, "This is what I'm doing."

I loved that statement and found inspiration in the simplicity and honesty of accepting ownership and responsibility. I admired the way he gave himself permission to not know, to explore, to be curious, to turn inward and listen with trust, rather than to continue seeking "out there" for direction and guidance and instruction.

I immediately recognized what he said as the inspiration I was looking for, and I embraced his statement as my own declaration, not only in martial arts but also in life. I embraced going back to basics, trusting inner wisdom, listening rather than imposing, taking responsibility for choices. It reminds me of when my grandson was a headstrong baby and his great grandmother wryly observed, "He is the captain of his ship." He was indeed.

As are we. In every moment, with every breath, we choose how we will live. So own it. Take responsibility for your life, without apology. It is liberating and empowering. It is grounding in a time of uncertainty and anxiety. It is a reassurance that we are enough. This is where true freedom lies.

This is what I'm doing.

"I Just Like To Do Things My Own Way"

Another example of someone who owns his choices is my son James. James is autistic. For those familiar with the spectrum, he would probably fall somewhere at the very low end of high functioning. Several years ago, I had a conversation with him about his adult life. I was trying to ask in a sensitive, diplomatic way, but was probably more inept and clumsy, how he felt about not being able to do some things that he might see other adults doing. I wondered if he saw himself as different, and if so, how he felt about it.

James thought for a minute and then he shrugged. "I just like to do things my own way."

So true. He does. He has always marched to the beat of his own drum, and happily, at least when allowed to march unimpeded.

When he was a boy, I once asked him what he wanted to be when he grew up.

"A deer!" he said. Not the sort of career choice answer I was expecting.

"I'm pretty sure you are going to be a man when you grow up," I replied.

"NOOOOOOOOO!!!!!!"

Looking back, I can see so many times along the way when I tried to make James fit into a mold. I believed that being a good mother to James meant trying to help him overcome the difficulties that I saw facing him. It meant making him more like everyone else.

Then one day, I passed by the bathroom door close enough to hear James talking to himself in the mirror.

"It's great to be James!"

Wow, I thought. Isn't this how all parents want their kids to feel? I now regret all the ways that I became the impediment to James's happy dance of life.

This is not an isolated example. How many ways do I do this to others? To myself? How many ways have I tried to mold myself into the person I thought I should be at the expense of the person within longing to be free?

We want others to agree with us, to act like we think they should act, to believe what we believe. We also want them to like us. We hold others and most of all ourselves to a standard conformity. And meanwhile, the natural universe of beauty and energy and wild variation longs to express itself through all of us and each of us.

The Universe just likes to do things its own way. And who are we to interfere?

The Universe is saying: "Allow me to flow through you unrestricted, and you will see the greatest magic you have ever seen."
~Klaus Joehle

Growing Asparagus

Ken Kesey is a great example of owning what you are doing. Renowned author and 1960s counterculture icon, in his later years he led a quiet life in rural Oregon. When asked by an interviewer during this time what he was doing to make the world a better place, he looked out from his front porch over the fields and said, "This year I'm growing asparagus."

One morning, someone expressed to me a feeling that many of us can relate to: a general sense of anxiety and despair over the world situation. What can we do, he asked, to make things better? Indeed. Just asking the question can create an overwhelming wave of helpless frustration. This is an un-answerable question on a global scale, at least for most of us.

Einstein said, "Problems cannot be solved with the same mindset that created them." And therein lies the problem. For example, we try to solve through politics issues that are fun-damentally entwined in our political process. It won't work. Nor will we solve through politics issues that are inherently not political.

Am I suggesting that we throw up our hands and go sulk in the corner, or start packing for that remote tropical island? Not at all. In fact, I'm not suggesting that we "do" anything in particular. I'm suggesting that we look at things differently, that we look without judgment, without seeking a solution. Instead, we can seek understanding, not of the world, but of ourselves.

Take me, for example. Like some, I watch with dismay an increasing polarity of us/them separation in the world. And as I watch more deeply, I begin to question how separation might be seeping into my own life.

When have I dismissed someone's opinion, for example, while bemoaning the lack of respect in political debate? When have I tried to win, while being disgusted with the whatever-it-takes-to-win campaign strategies? When have I walked past someone in need, while demonizing policies that seem heartless? When have I failed to be a good steward of my resources, while I rail at the lack of commitment to environ-mental and financial reform? When have I denied someone's experience, while protesting the insensitivity of stereotypical characterizations?

Humbling.

So what am I doing to make the world a better place? This year, I'm growing self-awareness.

*This capacity to align with your innate trust
brings you back in harmony with
the entire unfolding of the cosmos.*
~Jason Gregory

Living in a Goal Free Zone

As we shift from a life driven by fear to a life resting in trust, we've been exploring the freedom to make choices and the attendant responsibility for those choices. How do we make choices based in trust? How do we remove the blocks to our inner guidance? Overcoming fear is an obvious one of course. But there are other, more subtle ways that we interfere with our direct line to wisdom.

For example, western culture, at least in the United States, is very goal oriented. We make New Year's resolutions. We have five-year business and personal plans. My sons, who both have autism, have a meeting every year with service providers to set goals for the year with measurable checkpoints during the year. Many of our lives are structured this way, with large and small identified goals and measurable steps. We set goals, work towards our goals, achieve our goals, and bask in the success of having done so. Then we set new goals and start the process again.

Goals are associated with progress, accomplishment, hard work, even good character. They are encouraged, and those who set them and achieve them are admired. There is nothing wrong with that. Goals serve a purpose. But when we have blinders on that allow us to see only the goal-oriented path ahead, I wonder what opportunities we miss. Some of the best things that have happened in my life were not on my goal trajectory. In fact, more often than not, they completely derailed my goal progress.

For example, when I moved to Portland, I had a very specific job goal in mind. I began to search for leads that would take me in that direction. When someone mentioned a temporary job opportunity that was not goal related, I almost dismissed it. Then I decided I would take that job to provide some income while I looked for the job I really wanted. The first day of the temporary job, I went home amazed that someone was paying me to have so much fun. When the temporary period was up, I figuratively chained myself to the gate until they decided to keep me. Twenty years later, I retired from a job that continued to be fun and deeply rewarding.

On the personal front, I was living a full and busy life as a single parent with two kids. I had all I could handle, or so I thought. My goals targeted balancing home and work while meeting the needs of my autistic son and making sure that my daughter had her needs met as well. My goals definitely did not include more kids. And yet, suddenly there was my son's classmate, also autistic, who, for reasons beyond the scope of this book, was in crisis and needed a family to care for him. So, for reasons even further beyond the scope of this book and far beyond any rational explanation, I took him. And his presence has now blessed our family for many years in ways I never could have planned or anticipated.

Those are major life examples, but similar things happen to us all the time in big and small ways. At some point I realized that when I was not focused on goals, things that needed to get done still did, often in a more natural, organic way than when forced. I began to trust that life would lead me, and that when I was aligned in harmony with an open, receptive attitude, my path forward would become clear. And if it didn't, then I knew to wait until it did.

When people ask me these days what my goals are, I have a hard time coming up with any. It seems to me that they get in the way rather than provide helpful direction. Sure, I make plans. I go to the store with a list in hand, and my calendar has appointments to attend. The difference, perhaps, is that my life is not driven by personally selected goals as much as carried by the current of divine energy that flows through all creation. (That's actually a lot more practical than it sounds!)

Being driven by goals sometimes has a quality of anxiety that on some level seeks to control external circumstances and outcomes. Following life's labyrinth, on the other hand, has a quality of trust that rests in the assurance that our path leads us unerringly to our destination. Life is more enjoyable, relaxed, responsive. And when changes and challenges come, as they surely will, they can be met with resilience rather than struggle.

It's a relief to know that I don't have to plan and control every step in my life. That was exhausting!

For in the sacredness of every moment, Divine Grace
is telling you alone all that is required.
~Jean-Pierre de Caussade

Doing Everything while Doing Nothing

The sage does nothing, yet nothing is left undone.
~Dao De Jing

Our concern about jettisoning all our goals is that we will just become do-nothing sloths, lying on the couch until we are evicted for not paying our rent or mortgage. Not so. The concept of *wu wei* (non-action) is a theme throughout the *Dao De Jing*, one that has had people scratching their heads for millennia. In our overscheduled, never caught up, always behind, time managed, too tired to relax way of life, we accept as normal a pervasive sense of never accomplishing enough. The finish line is always just out of reach, no matter how fast or how far we run. It's a trap, like a fixed game we keep trying to win but never will. *Wu wei* offers another way.

Taken literally, *wu wei* does appear to grant us license to sit on the couch all day eating chips and ice cream while binge watching our favorite show. The kids are hungry and the dog needs to go outside? Sorry, I'm too busy lounging around being enlightened.

That doesn't seem right. For one thing, it ignores the second part of the quote—nothing is left undone. So I can do nothing and all the items on my to do list will get checked off? It must be magic because most of us can't even get through our to do lists when we're frantically doing stuff nonstop till we drop.

What's the secret?

An energy healer showed me an answer. After noticing that he had not mentioned or used a particular healing technique for a long time, I asked him, "Do you still do X?" He smiled with a slight shrug and replied, "X still happens."

That is what *wu wei* looks like in our daily lives. When we act without identifying with our actions, when we refrain from claiming success or failure, when our egos are not invested in a particular outcome, then we are able to see, really see, what is happening or not happening in the present moment, and we can discern what is necessary or appropriate in any given situation. We can respond and adapt, or rather, responding and adapting "happen." We quit struggling with the natural pace and rhythm of our lives and move in harmony with what is happening right now.

It doesn't mean that we don't make plans or have routines or responsibilities. It means that we can attend to what is necessary without judgment or inner conflict, without the effort of trying to force things to be a certain way. *Wu wei* doesn't mean that stuff doesn't get done, but it changes our thinking about who is doing it and our relationship to what is being done. We think less about "I" until "I" simply fades into the flow of life, no matter whether our lives flow like raging rapids or meandering streams. We learn to trust that we don't have to do everything in order for what is necessary to get done.

To me, *wu wei* is not so much about non-action as it is about non-interference. When we give up our need to control everything and allow the natural flow of energy to flow through us, life is easier. That doesn't mean that challenges don't arise. It doesn't mean that we like everything that happens or that we are indifferent. It means that we engage directly with what is instead of struggling with how we want things to be. So when we catch ourselves struggling, we can pause and ask ourselves what is really going on. Chances are we will realize that we have shifted from trust to fear. Take a breath, listen within, and trust your inner wisdom guide you.

With nothing to do she does nothing. With all things
to do, she accomplishes all things—yet sees not a trace
of distinction between these.
~Paul Ferrini

Courage To Trust

*Courage is not simply one of the virtues, but the form
of every virtue at the testing point.*
~C. S. Lewis

At the testing point, courage is what transcends fear and keeps
our hearts open. An open heart allows other virtues to manifest, even in the most challenging times. Courage empowers
us to trust. The word courage comes from Old French "corage,"
which in turn comes from the Latin "cor" meaning heart.
Although there can be some overlap, as when first responders
put themselves in danger to rescue someone, it's not exactly
the same as daring or boldness. Courage can also be quiet.

Courage is what enabled a little girl sitting in a restaurant
with her family not only to feel compassion for the homeless
man on the bench outside, but to pick up her plate and take
her dinner to him.

Courage is what enabled a popular guy in high school to
be kind to a girl with disabilities and ask her to the prom.

Courage is what enabled a protester to walk up and hug
a police officer, and what allowed the police officer to hug
her back.

Courage is what enabled the Amish community to forgive
the man who came into one of their schools and shot ten
little girls.

Courage is not limited to humans. When my dog Rosie
was a puppy, she was so terrified of other dogs that I could not
take her for a walk. So I went to a wonderful trainer for help.
We played in a big empty room until Rosie felt comfortable.
Then the trainer brought in a huge old collie. The collie just
lay down in a big furry heap, completely ignoring the little
fluff ball freaking out in the corner.

Rosie circled, alert and anxious. After a few minutes, she slowly approached the collie from the back, step by careful step. As she got closer, leaning forward to check out this mountain of dozing canine, stretching out her nose as far as she could without falling over, the trainer kept praising her in a high baby voice. "So brave, Rosie. So brave."

Rosie was indeed being brave. Not Lassie running into a burning building to save Timmy brave, but taking one tiny timid step closer to what scared her brave. That old collie was her testing point. And in the fertile soil of her courage, trust sprouted and eventually bloomed.

Some of us do not recognize the courage it takes to see things as they are, to see ourselves as we are. We are brave when we admit we are afraid, when we offer compassion to a stranger, when we are generous with our time, when we give ourselves permission to have healthy boundaries, when we stay with our practice in challenging times, when we forgive ourselves and others, when we pause to take a breath before reacting, when we trust in the basic goodness of the universe.

We can be the heroes of our own lives when we realize that we are at a testing point and we choose to trust. "So brave, so brave."

I have seen everything
I have no fear
I have the heart of a lion
I shine like Venus
~Rumi

PART 2

THE PRACTICE OF AWAKENING

CHAPTER 4

Our Eternal Practice

Restoring enlightenment is our eternal practice.
~Dao De Jing

Some of us engage in spiritual practices hoping to become something we want to be, something we think we're not. We seek to transform ourselves into some ideal that we fear we will never attain. In fact, we never will "attain" it because we seek to become who we already are. Our seeking obscures the awareness of our true nature. It's like a baby bird who might practice flying but doesn't need to practice being a bird. We don't need to become someone else; we need to remember who we already are, the enlightened beings that we always have been and always will be.

When we speak of spiritual practices, then, if we are not practicing to attain enlightenment, what exactly are we practicing? As the quote above reminds us, we practice restoring enlightenment rather than attaining it. We practice allowing our true nature to naturally unfold and manifest, just as an acorn naturally grows into an oak tree.

The Chinese character for "practice" occurs only once in the entire *Dao De Jing* in a line that says, "This is our eternal practice." The character 習 is composed of a top part meaning feathers or wings, and a bottom part meaning white or pure. To me, this suggests an image of our practice lifting us up on white wings to return us to our pure and natural state of enlightenment.

So what are the eternal practices that liberate us from all that holds us in bondage to our illusion of separateness and lack? There are many practices that go by just as many different names. When someone asks me what the best practice is, I respond that the best practice is the one you will actually do. Because when we empty our cups and step forward in trust, all spiritual practices awaken in us a remembrance of who we are and return us to the promised land of home.

Bodyfulness

Everything you'll ever need to know is within you; the secrets of the universe are imprinted on the cells of your body.
~Dan Millman

Spiritual practice often overlooks the body. However, in many cultures, the body is the place where the thought of separation begins and is thus the place where healing can initiate awakening. How strange that we are not taught to inhabit our bodies as spiritual beings. Instead, we are often taught either to identify only as a body, or alternatively, to reject the body.

The popular term "mindfulness" focuses on spiritual practices of the mind, so I'm using the term "bodyfulness" to focus on the embodiment of spiritual practice. Our bodies have much to teach us about life and how to live it. I used to think that my body was just something to carry my head around. But when I started practicing martial arts, I realized that I was not only learning about my body, but also learning from my body about my mind and spirit. My body was teaching me to integrate all parts into a harmonious whole.

It might seem counter-intuitive to start a spiritual practice chapter with the body, but you might be surprised to discover how much wisdom is contained in that mix of water and stardust held together in a bag of skin where your spirit has taken up residence for a while. A little humor doesn't hurt either:

> *The Church says: The body is a sin.*
> *Science says: The body is a machine.*
> *Advertising says: The body is a business.*
> *The Body says: I am a fiesta.*
> ~Eduardo Galeano

It Starts with the Breath

> *Breathe deeply, until sweet air extinguishes the burn*
> *of fear in your lungs and every breath is a beautiful*
> *refusal to become anything less than infinite.*
> ~D. Antoinette Foy

We can't talk about learning from our body without talking about breath. Indeed, that is the title and theme of this book. Some years ago, there was a popular book titled *All I Really Need to Know I Learned in Kindergarten*. I might rephrase that to say that all I really need to know I learned from breathing.

First of all, my body knows how to breathe. I don't need to instruct it or supervise it. I don't even need to understand how the breath works. Breathing teaches me how to trust the natural process that happens without any interference.

Breathing teaches me to live now, in this moment. We all understand that breathing keeps us alive. So do food and water. But unlike food and water, breathing keeps us alive in the present moment and only in the present moment. I can survive for a while on the food I ate this morning. But the breath I took five hours ago, or even five minutes ago, cannot keep me alive right now. The breath that keeps me alive is the one I'm taking as I write this sentence. Another breath keeps me alive as I write this one.

Breathing teaches me about the oneness of all life. Everything that is alive right now is breathing in one way or another. Our breath gives life to plants as they use the carbon dioxide we exhale, just like they in turn exhale the oxygen we require. So not only is all life connected, but all life is interdependent as we receive and generate the breath of life.

Breathing teaches me about impermanence. What begins in time will end in time. I breathed in when I was born, and I will breathe out when I die. We manifest into form, and we return to formlessness. Each individual breath is a reminder of the inevitable cycle of life and death.

Breathing teaches me about letting go. Breathing keeps me alive only when I release one breath to allow another. I cannot hold one breath while trying to stock up on the next one. Breathing is the best example of emptying our cup, as the Zen story goes, so that it can be filled again.

Breathing teaches me gratitude. I did nothing to deserve my breath. I didn't work to earn it. It is a gift, freely offered, lovingly bestowed, gratefully received.

Breath teaches me to relax. It is the original biofeedback technique. When we're born, we naturally breathe into our bellies. Over time many of us abandon the free, relaxed belly breathing of infants and children, and begin to breathe shallowly in our upper chests. This upper chest breathing tells our brains that we are in danger, creating a feedback loop of chronic anxiety. Conversely, breathing fully as our belly relaxes and expands tells our brains that we are safe. Thus, we can calm our anxiety and stress simply by allowing our bodies to return to their natural way of breathing.

As we learn from breath's wisdom, we are like the monk who said he was never not meditating. With every breath, we are never not practicing.

> *Breathing in, I calm body and mind. Breathing out, I smile. Dwelling in the present moment, I know this is the only moment.*
> ~Thich Nhat Hanh

"Find Your Vertical Line"

"Find your vertical line" was a favorite instruction from one of my martial arts teachers. As we moved through different postures and exercises, he often reminded us, "Where is your vertical line?" or "Find your vertical line."

This vertical line runs from the crown of our head straight through our body to the perineum, right between our legs. It goes by several names: center line, central channel, central axis, central equilibrium.

When our central channel is properly aligned and cleared of any blockages, a conduit is opened between heaven and earth, pulsing light and energy. We are in balance, grounded, moving freely and effortlessly. If you are a *Star Trek* fan, imagine the warp core, the energy source of the spaceship, usually pictured as a vertical cylinder pulsing with light.

A good way to align your central channel is to start with a good standing or sitting posture. Imagine that you are suspended from the top of your crown. Let your body use gravity to fall into a relaxed vertical position. Then find the center line running from the crown through the perineum. Extend that line vertically in both directions to connect yourself to heaven and earth. Your body can feel effortlessly supported by your structure.

As with many aspects of martial arts, this concept works just as well in daily life as it does in physical practice. Going through the inevitable unsettling shifts in life, we might feel confused, off balance, and out of sync. Anxiety takes our energy upwards into our heads, and we lose our connection to our body and our emotional ground or center.

This is where the benefit of practice shows up, isn't it? We practice for these times when we are caught off guard, knocked off balance, at the edge of our comfort zone, in pain, afraid. In other words, we practice in real life, as it is.

So I hear my teacher's words. Find your vertical line.

I find it first in my breath. Quiet, deep, slow, soft. Then in my body, standing or sitting in alignment, connecting to heaven and earth. When I sense my central channel aligned and open, then my body leads my emotions and my mind into balance. Energy pulses through the open channel. Yes, sadness may still be there, but in equilibrium with all other emotions. Fear is soothed with stillness. Agitation is cradled with compassion. Energy moves freely.

Until it doesn't.

And then I find my vertical line again.

Get yourself grounded and you can navigate even the
stormiest roads in peace.
~Steve Goodier

How to Calm DOWN When You Are Riled UP

We can use our groundedness and alignment practice when our emotions are churning, we are worried, or in some other way we are feeling off balance. What to do? The answer is right there in the words we use to describe ourselves when we are either upset or at ease. It is a matter of direction.

When we are angry or agitated, our energy rises. Our breathing is shallow, in the upper part of the chest. Our weight shifts forward and upward. Our attention is in our heads. Our thoughts run amok, shouting stories about whatever has initiated our distress. We fuel the stories with fiery emotions. Or perhaps we try to douse the fire with other thoughts, which keep us in our heads. So many terms identify this upward direction of energy. We get riled *up*, churned *up*, revved *up*, *up*set. Tempers *rise*.

Other words suggest a way to restore our inner equilibrium: calm *down*, settle *down*, slow *down*. The direction away from distress is downward. So how do we do that? Because we rely so much on our brains, our first instinct is to think our way out of a problem. However, thinking often *is* the problem. Our distress is in our thoughts. So instead of trying to think our way out of distress, a more direct way is to move out of our heads and down into our bodies.

Here is a simple exercise I use when I need to bring my energy down. I inhale and stand on my toes, raising my arms away from my body. I pause there a moment, then suddenly release my weight as I exhale and drop into my feet, letting my arms fall at the same time. I keep my knees relaxed so that when my heels hit the ground, there is a soft bounce, like I am shaking all the tension loose and letting it sink into the earth. I bring my attention down to my feet and focus on their connection to the earth.

When my energy is more settled, then I can attend to restoring balance.

Finding Inner Balance

Developing an inner awareness of balance and alignment when things are calm helps us maintain equanimity in trying times. Try this experiment. See if you can balance on one foot.

If you can't balance on one foot, keep practicing, maybe with a chair or table or wall close by for support. Try to balance just for a few seconds. Increase your time as you get comfortable. Don't get overly ambitious—the point is not to fall! This is an exercise in listening to and working with your body, not forcing it beyond its limits.

If you can balance comfortably on one foot, make it more challenging. Can you move the raised foot and maintain balance? Can you turn your head to look in a different direction? Here's a tough one: while you are still on one foot, close your eyes. Does that affect your balance? For most of us, the answer is yes.

When I started practicing this exercise with my eyes closed, I got wobbly pretty fast. I realized how connected my sense of balance was to my visual field. This fascinated me. How is it, then, that visually impaired people can balance themselves? Clearly, their balance orientation is not dependent on being able to see their surroundings. There must be a way to find balance based on an internal orientation. Indeed, over time I discovered that by turning my awareness within, I could find my balance through the connection of my feet to the earth, and by using my sense of vertical alignment throughout my body to make the adjustments necessary to maintain balance.

Sometimes circumstances in my life are unsettling, unclear, and unknown, leaving me feeling unbalanced emotionally and energetically. I realized that, just like with my physical balance, I was looking externally to find my inner balance, my inner equanimity. I was wanting clarity of understanding and certainty of resolution concerning an external situation in order to feel peace within.

Once again, the body is my teacher. Just as I've learned that my body can balance itself without external orientation, I've learned that when life circumstances are unsettling emotionally and energetically, I can find inner balance by turning my awareness within. I can sense the adjustments that need to be made to restore equanimity without requiring my external circumstances to be a certain way.

Like with physical balance, inner balance is not a static state. Adjustments are made constantly in response to, and in harmony with, the movement of energy through our lives. Inner balance is a dance. Listen to the music of the universe that sings in your soul…and then close your eyes.

What you have been taught by listening to others'
words you will forget very quickly. What you have
learned with your whole body you will remember for
the rest of your life.
~Gichin Funakoshi

Quietness

In the forest still and true
One can hear a snowflake fall
Or resting among meadow flowers
The whisper soft of fairy wings
Turn within and one can hear
The rhythm of the heartsong drum
Go deeper down and listen listen
Can you hear it?
God is humming all creation

As we integrate the wisdom teachings of our bodies, we can become more open to the wisdom teachings of our souls. The practice of quietness is described in the *Dao De Jing* as closing the mouth. This of course could literally mean not talking. And certainly many of us, me included, sometimes talk when we should be listening. It could also, and perhaps more importantly, mean internal quietness, letting our thoughts settle like silt in murky water until the mind is clear and pure, until we can hear the voice of wisdom within.

In silence
The soul peeks out
To say hello

W.A.I.T.—Why Am I Talking?

Silence is the doorway to wisdom divine.
~The Way of Mastery

The easiest way to think about quietness is to contrast it with talking out loud. When my kids were growing up, I tended to talk on and on when I was upset with them. At some point, long after listening had stopped, my son would hold up his hand palm out in a stop signal and say in a robotic voice, "Talking...is...over."

What is this need to talk really about? To contemplate this, we need to stop talking long enough to listen, not only to others but to ourselves. We need to be aware of the discomfort that underlies the urge to speak. Then we can explore the nature of that discomfort instead of escaping from it with spoken words. I suspect that a good part of our motivation to talk isn't really about the content of what we are saying. Perhaps we talk because we are looking for connection. We want to be heard. We want to feel valued. We want to not feel alone.

If we could hear that underlying need in others, and recognize it in ourselves, perhaps our speech would begin to serve a purpose of genuine connection rather than grasping for relief. The acronym W.A.I.T.—Why Am I Talking—is a wonderful reminder to pause and gently question our use of words. Before I speak, perhaps I could ask myself: Is what I'm about to say an improvement on silence?

If I can answer yes, then I might extend an open hand palm up to my son and say in a human voice, "Communicating… has… just… begun."

> *Never miss a good chance to shut up.*
> ~Will Rogers

Rest

> *I think 99 times and find nothing. I stop thinking,*
> *swim in silence, and the truth comes to me.*
> ~Albert Einstein

When we begin to quiet our urge to speak aloud, we'll discover that much of the unending "talking" is in our thoughts. Our minds are jabbering away, sometimes in our conscious thoughts, but mostly in the background of our awareness. This was made clear to me one day when I woke up with a migraine. I took some medicine and went back to bed with a cold gel pack on my forehead. The headache did not subside. It got worse.

As I lay there, I became aware of the constant chatter going on in my mind. We all have that background thinking loop that plays and replays behind our conscious and directed thinking. My mind, when left to its own devices, explores the most random locations, relives the past, rehearses the future, ponders plots from TV shows, imagines dire events unlikely to ever happen, picks at emotional scabs until they bleed, and considers strategies to manipulate uncontrollable people and circumstances. Basically, it never stops talking.

When the migraine pain shut down my conscious thinking, my attention was free to observe what was really going on underneath. What I hadn't realized before was how energy depleting it is to run this ceaseless program in the background of our minds. It's like the drain on our electric power when we leave things plugged in that we aren't using. I could actually feel the energy seeping out of me.

And even more surprising was how painful these thoughts were. With the hypersensitivity of the migraine, I could physically feel the impact of each thought firing in my brain. The sparking neurons felt like countless tiny spikes being hammered inside my head.

Naturally, I wanted it to stop. I tried to make it stop. No luck. I felt a little panicky at the relentlessness of this habitual monologue. And then I heard a soft voice gently saying, "Rest." For a moment, everything quieted. Relief. It started back up almost immediately, but now I knew what to do. I stopped listening to it, stopped fighting with it, and silently whispered "rest," tenderly, lovingly, like a mother soothing a restless baby. Again, rest ... rest ... rest. For moments at a time, my mind quieted. The pain of the migraine was still present, but there was a spaciousness about it, a peace. I rested with the pain, and with the reminders to my brain to rest with me.

Since then, I've been more aware of this chatter. During meditation I bring my wandering mind home with the reminder to "rest." When going through my day, as I start to get hooked by the drama of the moment, I can remember to let my mind rest. Even if the quietness only lasts a moment or two, we can pause to enjoy a spacious silence.

> *The most valuable thing we can do for the psyche,*
> *occasionally, is to let it rest, wander, live in the*
> *changing light of room, not try to be or do*
> *anything whatever.*
> ~May Sarton

Doing Nothing in the Right Way

Our bodies can teach us a lot about quietness. One summer I got a brutal but thankfully brief stomach bug. Although the symptoms lasted only an afternoon and evening, it wiped me out so thoroughly that for the next few days all I could do was lie in bed eating ice chips. Even after I was sort of upright again, doing the simplest things wore me out.

After several days, I dragged myself to a martial arts class. When I explained to my teacher that I was on my feet for the first time in days, he told me to take it easy and just do what I could. I lasted only a minute or two of the warm-up exercises before having to sit down. After a while, I joined the class in a standing meditation. As soon as I got myself properly aligned and relaxed into the posture, energy suddenly bubbled up inside me—whoosh! It was like I had a low battery and someone plugged me into a super fast charger. By the time the meditation ended a few minutes later, I felt as close to normal as I had in days and felt fine for the rest of class.

Later I told the teacher what had happened as a result of simply standing still in alignment. "Sometimes doing nothing in the right way is the best thing," he replied.

That is a pretty amazing statement, especially in our "do, do more, do better" culture. It made me think about how I might listen to a friend without offering advice or trying to fix things. Or not react when someone is rude or trying to pick a fight. Or step back when a child needs to learn about consequences or how to solve a problem independently.

My body taught me that pushing through or forcing is not always what is called for. Doing nothing in the right way allows the energy to expand naturally and move freely, which is often the best thing for all concerned.

> *Don't just do something, sit there!*
> ~Sylvia Boorstein

Listening with Your Whole Self

You will find me in the silence...

When we practice quietness, we listen in the silence. Listening in the silence means not only listening with our ears but listening with our whole self.

One of the governing skills cultivated in tai chi is a Chinese word "ting" that means listen but has a broader meaning than its English equivalent. In developing "ting" when we practice with a partner, we "listen" to our partner's energy not with our ears but through touch, sensing beyond the point of contact to "hear" everything within the partner's body of energy.

The Chinese character on the next page gives us insight into this deep form of listening, not just in tai chi practice but in our lives.

聽

When we break the character into its components, we see on the upper left side 耳, meaning ear, and below that 王, meaning ruler. But remember that in ancient times the ruler was considered the intermediary between heaven and earth, as we can see from the three horizontal lines representing heaven and earth, with the ruler or humankind in the center, connected all together with the vertical line. So these two parts, ear and ruler, convey a sense of listening in alignment with heaven and earth.

On the right side of the character, we see on top 直, meaning upright, straight, or correct. It's made up of ten 十 and eyes 目, suggesting clear vision or inner vision. Below that is 心, meaning heart.

When we put this all together, the richness of meaning emerges. I like to think it means something like "listening in alignment with heaven and earth to the inner wisdom of the heart." This kind of listening is deep, holistic listening, activating our body, mind, and spirit. It is listening to what is beyond words. Like the shadow of a tree is not the tree, like the swaying of meadow grass is not the breeze, like a finger pointing at the moon is not the moon, words suggest truth, but are not truth.

And what might we hear when we listen with our whole selves? The song of creation humming in our souls, vibrating us into form from the mystery of Oneness, and calling us back into the eternal embrace of the Beloved.

Put your ear down close to your soul and listen hard.
~Anne Sexton

Allowing

Transformation is allowed. Allowing is practiced.

Within the quietness, we make space for whatever arises and allow it to arise without our interference. Allowing can be misunderstood as standing back and doing nothing, like overly permissive parents who let their kids run amok. I don't think that's it. I think of allowing as refraining from judgment as life opens up within and around us. We act or refrain from acting as part of a natural unfolding, an appropriate response to the present moment rather than an attempt to control or direct things from a place of fear or worry. Allowing is rooted in our willingness to trust our natural alignment with the sacred flow of the universe.

> *I should be there*
> *Not here*
> *Yet here I am*
> *I should be that*
> *Not this*
> *Yet this I am*
> *I am here*
> *And I am this*
> *It is enough*

The Nature of Allowing

Allowing is practiced by accepting reality as it is, accepting ourselves as we are. When I struggle, resist, try to control something or someone, or judge anything (especially myself),

I can be sure that somewhere in there is an opportunity to practice allowing.

Einstein said that we choose to believe that we live in either a friendly universe or a hostile universe. That's another way of saying that we can choose to trust the Universe to manifest its own perfect nature and to embrace us in its flowing current. We can trust our inner wisdom to vibrate in harmonic resonance with this current and to guide us in perfect alignment with its movement.

As with any practice, we get better over time. Allowing becomes integrated into how we engage with our lives. It becomes a habit. There is a sense of effortlessness, wonder, humility, gratitude. The transformation of our lives unfolds naturally. We recognize, to paraphrase the Bible, that we are part of a universe marvelously and wonderfully made. We remember who we are and live into the truth of our being. Allowing becomes our life art.

> *All suffering is the resistance of Reality. All*
> *awakening and healing is the letting go of resistance.*
> *Forgiveness. Allowance.*
> ~The Way of Mastery

Trying Blocks Allowing

Before exploring ways to practice allowing, it might be helpful to explore what is *not* helpful. "Try, try again," is a phrase many of us grew up with. There are many other familiar encouragements to make more effort, get back on your feet, try your best, don't give up. There is nothing wrong with trying, and it is essential in certain contexts. But in the practice of allowing, it can be a hindrance.

For example, in martial arts trying is a double-edged sword (pun intended). Once, when I was practicing with another student before class, the teacher was watching us from across the room. After a few minutes, he called to me, "You're trying too hard."

Sigh. Like I hadn't heard THAT before! Many times....

Only a few months before that, I was practicing with a different teacher. All my efforts were easily and immediately turned to my disadvantage. Seeking some advice, I said, "I'm trying to...."

The teacher interrupted before I could even finish the sentence. "That's your problem. You're trying."

Bruce Lee famously gave this advice in an interview about his martial arts style: "Be water, my friend." Water does not try. It doesn't struggle. It doesn't contend. It flows effortlessly in harmony with gravity and the contours of its environment. Nothing is softer; yet nothing is more powerful.

As in martial arts, so in life. This became evident when I asked to have a conversation with a friend. I thought this conversation would be beneficial for the friend, with me offering some insight about how to move forward through a challenging situation they faced. I had suggested opportunities to get together, and I had encouraged the other person to hear me out. But. The. Other. Person. Did. Not. Want. To.

I was trying too hard. Again.

Now, when I catch myself trying to make things conform to how I think things should be, I remember to take a deep breath and settle down. I wait. In the example about the conversation I was trying to have, I accepted that it would happen or it wouldn't. If it did, it would happen at the right time, and if I was paying attention and willing to release control, I would know what to say. I have learned that I can't control the outcome. I can only flow with the current and see where it takes me.

The Heaviness of History

*Those who do not remember the past
are condemned to repeat it.*
~George Santayana

Oops, I did it again.
~Britney Spears

In addition to trying, another hindrance to the practice of allowing is all the history we drag with us like heavy baggage. Many of us have caught ourselves at one time or another repeating a pattern or a mistake, and thinking, "I knew better. Why did I do that again?" Our history can teach us to make better choices if we learn from it.

However, our history can also be a burden that we carry with us, weighing us down with hurts that remain unforgiven, regrets that torment us, failings that shame us, roads not taken that tease us with fantasy. We sometimes base much of our identity on history in a way that confines us and limits us. We might identify with a difficult family dynamic, challenges we faced in school, relationships that ended, a cultural environment that expected us to conform. We can be trapped by the narrative of our life.

By the time we've gotten to a certain age, we have a lot of history to remember. I wonder if we can remember it and learn from it without dragging it behind us or being caged by it. Can we embrace the lessons as well as the gifts with gratitude, bless all our stories, and release them to the past so that we can liberate our present and future moments?

Emotional Hoarding

Along with our baggage of history, we also hoard emotions that weigh us down. But what if we are told, as Adyashanti said, that the price of living an awakened life is giving up every reason we have to stop loving? Every judgment, every resentment, every hurt feeling, every unforgiving thought, every irritation, every criticism, every "othering," no matter how justified, keeps us locked in an emotional state of suffering. Giving them up, all of them, without exception, will free us to live a more integrated, harmonious, healthier, happier, awakened life.

Most of us, if we're honest, can discover an emotional closet full of clutter, or at least an emotional junk drawer. When we look, we might be able to toss some things, but there will be that one little thing that we hold in our hand with hesitation. "You never know when I might need that," we think. Or there might be the emotional treasure that is displayed in a place of honor on the mantel. Such a spot is often reserved for the big unforgivable attachments we never forget: parents who let us down, lovers who left us, friends who betrayed us. Who can argue with those reasons to stop loving? No one.

That's the point, isn't it? I can justify every reason I have to stop loving. I can hold on to it in perfect righteousness. And I can wear my resultant suffering like a cloak of justice. A heavy cloak that drags with the weight of accumulated wrongs I can't let go of.

So why can't we just unfasten that cloak and leave it in the dirt? Do we hold on because of some fear of what will happen if we let it go? Would we feel grief or vulnerability? Or perhaps, if we look closely, we might admit there is some delicious pleasure in sitting in judgment, in fantasizing revenge, in attracting sympathy from others for our injury.

Whatever our reason, we will hold on to it until we want freedom more than we want to suffer. This is really a straightforward cost/benefit analysis. Do we want to keep holding on to resentment even at the price of our joy and contentment? Maybe the answer is yes. In that case, hoard away, but do it with the awareness of the price we are choosing to pay. On the other hand, we might determine that we are willing to let it go, trusting that the relief we experience will outweigh the pleasure of righteous judgment.

The choice is ours.

> *Some people believe holding on and hanging in there*
> *are signs of great strength. However, there are times*
> *when it takes much more strength to know when to let*
> *go and then do it.*
> ~Ann Landers

A Burden Bowl

If we can't release our baggage of history or our hoarded emotions permanently, maybe we can just set them down for a little while. When the contemplation group I lead used to meet in person (pre-Covid), I sometimes placed a bowl by the door. As people entered, I invited them to place in the bowl anything that was weighing them down, distracting them, keeping them from being fully present: worries, anxiety, shoulds, judgments, have to's, and so on. I would assure everyone, "When we are finished, you can pick them back up on your way out, or you can leave them in the bowl."

Most of us, I imagine, could think of a few burdens we would like to leave in the bowl for a little respite. One burden I have been carrying around for a long time is guilt for pain that I caused in a friendship. I have come to understand, however, that there is nothing more I can do. I have listened, I have acknowledged and apologized, and I have made what amends I can. I can't go back and redo anything in the past, nor can I offer anything in the present that will undo what is already done. It's time to lay this burden down.

This does not mean I no longer feel compassion. On the contrary, releasing my burden of guilt frees me to care more deeply about the other person. My heart is more open to love without the shackles of judgment, judgment of the other person for how they handle their pain, judgment of myself for my part in causing it. Blame and judgment go into the bowl along with guilt.

The idea of a burden bowl is an invitation to leave behind what no longer serves us. Along with guilt, I might place in the burden bowl judgment, resentment, pride, fear, self-consciousness, criticism, impatience, control, and more. And with each weight I release, I feel my spirit grow lighter and brighter.

May today be the day we lay our burdens down and walk through the door of liberation, freeing ourselves from the unnecessary weight, opening our hearts with infinite compassion, humbling us with blessings of grace, uniting us with the breath of life that we share with all living things.

> *You wanna fly, you got to give up the shit*
> *that weighs you down.*
> ~Toni Morrison

Bless and Release

As we have seen, the practice of allowing involves a lot of letting go. Sometimes, even when we understand and desire the relief of letting go, the hardest burden to release is a challenging relationship. It's hard to be at peace or to keep an open heart when we feel hurt, irritated, enraged, judgmental, or frightened. It's easy to justify our own feelings and reactions. After all, this other person did or said (fill in the blank).

We want the other person to see things our way, to admit that they are wrong, and thus of course, to acknowledge that we are right. We want them to behave differently, to be the way we want them to be, and thus to alleviate our own discomfort and distress. We want them to see us the way we want to be seen, and to love us the way we want to be loved. And we blame them when they don't.

The Way of Mastery reminds us that we cannot control what someone else thinks or says or does. Instead of trying to control what we can't control, we are encouraged to bless the other person and "release them to have the perceptions that they would choose." It's like the catch and release method of fishing. We "catch" the person on the hook of our judgment, and then "release" them with a blessing. Or we could flip that around because we are really catching ourselves on the hook of our judgment and releasing ourselves through offering a blessing.

This concept of bless and release breaks the mental thought cycle of frustration and hurt feelings, and creates space to breathe. I feel liberated from my own habitual discontent and futile efforts to make things different, which of course means making the other person different. Instead, the practice of bless and release makes *me* different. It restores peace, if not between me and another person, at least within my own spirit.

Until I'm caught again. Bless and release. As many times as it takes.

*To forgive is to set a prisoner free and discover that the
prisoner was you.*
~Lewis B. Smedes

The Sadness of Letting Go

*All changes, even the most longed for, have their
melancholy; for what we leave behind us is a part of
ourselves; we must die to one life before
we can enter another.*
~Anatole France

Allowing involves release, and any letting go is a loss, even if the release is voluntary and perhaps a relief. We expect to experience grief when a loved one dies, when a relationship ends, when illness strikes. We might not be so quick to recognize the veil of sadness that drapes our shedding of outgrown beliefs or ideas.

As we practice allowing, we release the things we thought we knew: our beliefs about what is good or bad, our certainty about how things should be, even our definition of who we are. A moment of awakening is liberating. And while it is often a moment of transcendent joy, you might find yourself looking back at the receding shore with a touch of compassion and nostalgia, because you know that "chopping wood and carrying water," as the saying goes, will never be the same.

When you go through a transition, even one that you sought and greatly want, it's okay to give yourself permission to acknowledge the loss, to allow the sadness, to honor what is left behind, to thank whoever and whatever has brought you to this moment. Allowance judges nothing, excludes nothing, but rather welcomes everything, *everything*, with the tender touch of love and a humble bow of gratitude.

Whispering, "Thank you."

> *No one tells you*
> *There is a sadness*
> *When all is left behind*
> *Although shed willingly*
> *Touch lingers*
> *A last caress*
> *Of what was once a treasure*
> *There is no going back*
> *Nor would you want to*
> *Yet there were moments*
> *When happiness kissed your lips*
> *And longing stirred your soul*
> *When the dream sang sweetly*
> *And illusion beckoned beauty*

Not This, Not This—This Too, This Too

These apparently contradictory phrases are at the heart of many wisdom teachings, representing the two aspects of the practice of allowing—release and acceptance. We've seen in this section that allowing involves releasing that which no longer serves us, and accepting, without judgment or the need to control, the reality of what is. These two phrases are little reminders to let go and allow.

"Neti, neti" is a Sanskrit expression from ancient Hindu texts. It can be translated as "Not this, not this." It reminds us to not latch onto beliefs and opinions, judgments and fears.

"This too, this too" is a phrase used by Thich Nhat Hanh, teaching us to accept what is, whether that is circumstances, feelings, even those opinions and judgments.

I find that acceptance rather than resistance is what allows me to soften my grip and release whatever binds me. If I make a mistake, as I do on rare occasions (!), I sometimes replay the situation endlessly, feeling worse and worse. But no matter how wise I am in hindsight about what I should have done, or wish I had done, I can't change what I did. I try to deny, rationalize, justify, reframe, tell a different story—anything other than just acknowledging that I made a mistake. So now not only have I made a mistake, but I have created a story about it evoking feelings of shame, embarrassment, anger, and judgment.

So I quit fighting with reality and accept what happened, without embellishment. This too, this too. And I accept my feelings of regret and sadness. This too, this too.

Everything is workable, everything becomes my teacher, everything has a place in my life.

When I can accept my circumstances and myself, as is, the thoughts that torment me begin to fade. I can see through them. They are not real. Neti, neti. Not this, not this. They do not bind me. They have no power over me. They no longer separate me from others. I need not defend my position, nor impose my views. I don't need to be right. Not this, not this.

Harmony is restored.

When I was in therapy, my therapist would often respond to my frequent descriptions of how I had somehow fallen short, or not been my best, with a tilt of her head and a little smile. "Welcome to the human race," she would say. I never liked her at those moments. Being part of the human race was not comforting or appealing. I held myself to a higher standard. "And how is that working for you?" was another one of her standard lines. I didn't like her then either, because of course, it wasn't working very well at all.

But now I am older, and if not wiser, certainly more tired. Too tired to struggle against what is. Too tired to pretend. Too tired to carry the heavy baggage of a lifetime of judgments and failings. Too tired to do anything other than the best I can do in this moment. Allowing becomes not just a practice, but a generous gift of relief.

No wonder sages are most often portrayed as old…or as Yoda.

For after all, the best thing one can do when it
is raining is let it rain.
~Henry Wadsworth Longfellow

Awareness

[A]nd the labor which they had to perform was to
look; and because of the simpleness of the way, or the
easiness of it, there were many who perished.
~1 Nephi 17:41, The Book of Mormon

This verse seems to rise up out of its surrounding context, put its hands on either side of my face, and speak directly to me. "Pay attention!" it gently commands. If quietness unlocks the door, and allowing invites all to enter, awareness looks to see who shows up.

Mindfulness is a popular practice these days. There are many ways to describe mindfulness. I think of it as awareness. We sometimes limit our concept of mindfulness to our thinking brains. Awareness, to me, is a broader term that expands to include more than mind. It's like a default setting of being present with our whole selves, with all our senses, physical, mental, and beyond. Once we enter the quietness and allow all things to arise in our experience, we embrace it all with our "looking" as we see things as they are.

> *Let us not look back in anger, nor forward in fear, but around in awareness.*
> ~James Thurber

If It's So Simple and Easy, Why Do Many "Perish"?

We sometimes look but often we don't see what's there. Instead of seeing what is, we see our thoughts about what is, our beliefs about what is, our judgments about what is, our stories about what is. We create an image with our thoughts and believe that what we think *is* what is.

Our reality becomes a closed system as we create our own illusion and then relate to it. We like our illusion and want to keep it, or we don't like it and want to change it. All the while, we've missed what actually is. We are not really looking. We are looking away.

So what does it mean to look? The verse says it is simple and easy. We don't have to acquire new skills or learn more information. On the contrary, looking, really looking, is a process of releasing, letting go of our beliefs and opinions and judgments long enough to see what is right in front of us in the present moment before we start telling ourselves a story.

If it's so simple and easy, why does it seem so hard? Why do so many "perish," as the verse says? Because we are so attached to our stories. Our stories are familiar and habitual. They have become so real to us that we are unaware of the illusions we have trapped ourselves in. As we saw in Chapter 2, we identify with our stories and they become who we think we are.

We can't really stop our brains from telling stories. This is what brains do. But we can bring our awareness to the present moment and look, really look, before the gap closes and our story begins. Once the story begins, we can observe it without becoming ensnared by it. We are free then to keep our attention on what is. We are free to look.

> *Those who seek should not stop seeking until they find. When they find, they will be disturbed. When they are disturbed, they will marvel, and will rule over all.*
> ~Gospel of Thomas

Zen Vacuuming

> *Life gives you plenty of time to do whatever you want to do if you stay in the present moment.*
> ~Deepak Chopra

"Looking" often involves slowing down enough to engage with the present moment without an agenda. When we are in a hurry, we pass by opportunities to marvel. Once, while visiting a gorgeous Japanese garden, I noticed a young man squatting in a patch of grass with his back toward me. I couldn't see what he was doing so I asked a nearby employee, who explained to me that he was cutting the grass with a small pair of scissors. I walked around the path till I could see that sure enough, he was doing just that. Quiet, content, snipping away, one green blade at a time.

I thought about that guy later when I was at my cabin. The cabin is nestled in the forest under huge evergreens that are always shedding their needles, which, no matter how often I vacuum, find their way inside and settle down on the rug, the floor, and the furniture.

When I noticed them scattered around one afternoon, I leaned down to pick up one or two, and then a few more. Before I knew it, instead of dragging the vacuum out, I was methodically moving around the room, calm and content, picking up pine needles. I wasn't in a hurry, and it seemed like a pleasant way to spend some time. It was meditative in a way, and oddly satisfying. Very Zen.

Why? I'm not sure. Maybe because I wasn't trying to be efficient or to achieve any particular result. I was just picking up pine needles. I wasn't irritated about them. I wasn't thinking of it as a chore. On the contrary, it became more like a little game, a hunt for hidden pine needles. It was fun. And then it was done. So simple.

I began to find other opportunities to not hurry through things that I had labeled chores. I washed a few dishes by hand, for example, feeling the heat of the soapy water, the weight and shape of the dish, the smooth gliding of the sponge over the surface, the rinse water cascading off. I emptied the dryer when the cycle was finished and put away my clean clothes promptly. I started making my bed every morning. I swept the front porch. I raked leaves with an actual rake, enjoying the rhythm and rustle, reminding me of pleasant childhood memories.

When I stopped thinking of all these things as chores to get through as quickly as possible, I found that I could be at peace with the activity rather than impatient. Disturbance gave way to marveling. And it no longer seemed like labor.

*I adore simple pleasures. They are the last refuge
of the complex.*
~Oscar Wilde

Practicing Awareness with Meditation

One way to help ourselves slow down and "look" is meditation. The benefits of meditation are by now widely known and accepted. However, many of us still don't have a regular meditation practice. The reasons vary. Maybe we think we have to be good at it, and we are afraid to fail. Maybe we are afraid we'll be successful and something unexpected or even scary will happen. Maybe we think something grand is supposed to happen, and if it doesn't we'll be disappointed.

One of the most common reasons for not meditating is that we think we don't have time to go somewhere special and sit on a cushion for an hour. But Eckhart Tolle reassures us that "one conscious breath in and out is a meditation." So simple.

I meditate for the simple reason that my life is better when I do. Not necessarily better each time, but overall. For the most part I meditate every day, but there are days that get skipped, and I don't fret about it.

Some people think that you should pick one style of meditation and stick to it, but I find benefit in some variety. One method I enjoy is a meditation practice called *zuo wang* in Chinese. *Zuo* means "sit" and *wang* means "forget," So the practice is literally "sit forget." At my age, this is so easy to do since I like to sit and I forget most things anyway!

The benefits of brief times devoted to meditation permeate my life. The line between "formal" meditation and daily life begins to blur. It reminds me of the encouragement in the Bible to "pray without ceasing." It doesn't mean that you should be kneeling with your head bowed all the time. That's not very practical. It means moving through your day with awareness and reverence. And that is very practical.

> *Meditation is the ultimate mobile device; you can use it anywhere, anytime, unobtrusively.*
> ~Sharon Salzberg

Training Ourselves Like a Puppy

If you have ever trained a puppy, one of the commands you might have taught is "watch." The objective is for the dog to lock eyes on you without being distracted by anything else, and wait for your next instruction.

We sometimes think of awareness as something to practice when our minds are not otherwise occupied. I've found, however, that awareness is most important to practice when our minds *are* otherwise occupied, distracted, anywhere else other than right here, now. When we keep our attention on the present moment, watching, waiting for our way to become clear, then things have a way of working out much better. We can learn to recognize the "squirrels" that dart across our mental path, and the temptation to look aside or give chase. We can learn to keep our mind trained on the moment.

Over and over again, the Universe teaches me this lesson. Something will happen and I will get distracted, turning my attention to a situation in order to change something, or more likely to "fix" something. Or perhaps my mind is just wandering off along paths of various narratives, rehashing the past, rehearsing the future. When this happens, I am no longer aware of the present moment. I am not open, listening, receptive to inner guidance, ready to respond. My inner eyes are elsewhere. I am restless, perhaps in distress. My soul asks for help. Again. And the Universe answers. Again.

Watch. Eyes on me. Only me. Wait for your way to be made clear. Be at peace.

The way is not in your thoughts. It is in your heart. It sings in your soul and resonates throughout your entire being. You will know it.

But only if you watch.

> *Your spirit knows who you are and what you're here*
> *to do. The heart is your inner knowing, the part of you*
> *that transcends mere emotions or intellect and sees*
> *and knows the path you need to follow.*
> ~Marnie Pehrson Kuhns

"You Are My Technique"

As we practice meditation or other ways of being aware, we find that we are more present, more spontaneously engaged in a natural way with each moment. I saw this demonstrated when I attended a martial arts workshop with a teacher visiting from California. This teacher was a small, slightly stooped, elderly Chinese man. He was explaining the way he responds to someone who is attacking him.

He demonstrated with a series of younger, bigger, stronger, martial arts experts. Time and time again, he deflected their attacks, and the attacker either fell backwards or fell forward past the teacher. The teacher didn't seem to exert much effort or even move that much. A flick of the wrist, a slight turn of the hips was all it took to render his attacker harmless.

Naturally, we were all amazed and somewhat mystified. One student asked him, "What is your technique?" He looked puzzled for a moment and then replied, "*You* are my technique." What he meant was that he does not have predetermined moves or countermoves. He remains empty and simply responds to what is presented to him.

"You are my technique" excites me because it suggests a way to approach so many situations in life. In a way, it is the art of active awareness. It encourages us to pay attention to what is, rather than to get caught up in our thoughts. We can work with circumstances in a natural, effortless way rather than trying to force them in a way that depletes our energy.

> *Use only that which works, and take it*
> *from any place you can find it.*
> ~Bruce Lee

The One in My Hand

Having "what is" as our "technique," and learning to keep our eyes on the present moment, leads us to a place of having no preference, no preconceived notions of what conditions are necessary to succeed.

If it hasn't become obvious already, I am a martial arts nerd. I love the art of combat (as opposed to actual combat!). Considering that among my favorite TV shows are *Vikings* and *Game of Thrones*, I suspect that in a former life, I was some sort of warrior...with a dragon.

Although not that skilled in martial arts myself, I like hanging out with folks who are. One day, while engaged in lively conversation comparing various weapons, I asked one of my teachers what his favorite weapon was. Without hesitation he answered, "the one in my hand." What an excellent martial arts lesson. We might not always have our nunchuku tucked in our back pocket or our sword hanging from our belt when the bad guys attack. Think of Jackie Chan picking up a mop or a shovel or a pool cue to use against an opponent.

But more than that, what a brilliant life lesson. Whatever situation we are faced with, it's no use wasting time wishing that circumstances were different. It is what it is, right then in the present moment. It is up to us to use what we have in that moment.

If, for example, I want to be happy, what good does it do to dream about some ideal situation? Sometimes we hold our happiness hostage to fantasy circumstances: I'll be happy when I'm on vacation, when I get a job, when I retire, when I have kids, when my kids move out, when I have a certain amount of money, when I have even more money, and so forth.

Or maybe I want to be enlightened, and I think that if I meditate a particular way, read a certain number of books, attend the right workshops, attach myself to the best teacher, and chant my mantra, then surely I will achieve awakening someday and live in bliss forevermore. Right? No, I will spend my life chasing illusion.

My teacher's answer about his favorite weapon reminds me that all I have in my hand is now, this moment. It's my favorite.

One who knows enough is enough
will always have enough.
~Dao De Jing

A Slogan for Practicing Awareness

Oh wow. Oh wow. Oh wow.
~Steve Jobs' last words before he died

That these were Steve Jobs' last words, or really anyone's last words, captures our imagination. A message from the threshold of death, from one perhaps seeing something marvelous, unable to describe it, simply expressing wonder.

We might think that the dying person is seeing what is beyond, what awaits us on the other side of death. I thought that too. But the more I contemplated this intriguing deathbed utterance, the more I considered the possibility that what he saw was not beyond death, unattainable by the living, but what has been here all along, what is here right now, available to us in every moment.

Most of us live our lives in the virtual reality of our thoughts, of the stories we tell ourselves. But we can choose differently. Not just different beliefs, or different lenses of perception, but to suspend belief and drop the lens. To see, as the Bible says, not through a glass darkly, but face to face.

How do we do that? Steve Jobs' last words offer a suggestion. WOW — Watch, Open, Wait.

Watch

Observe what is happening right here, right now. We can begin to awaken by watching… everything. Not everything we think is happening or should be happening, but what is really happening. This might be something external in our surroundings, or internal in our feelings or thoughts. Whatever it is, simply watch, like the puppy command.

Open

We can be curious rather than judgmental about what is happening. If we catch ourselves before we start telling a story about what is happening, we can recognize fear or anxiety or resistance, and breathe into it. This gives us space to relax and allow our evaluation, whether positive or negative, to fall away. Then we can be open to fully welcome the present moment, whatever it brings.

Wait

In the pause before jumping to a conclusion or taking action, we can release the need to know or understand or have a plan. Waiting in this context doesn't mean being passive, but rather alert. When we allow the way to reveal itself in its own time, we will know what to do, if anything, when the time is right to do it. Then doing will simply "happen."

When we follow these steps, our spirits are filled with wonder and gratitude. And the only response to that is...
Oh wow.

Be happy in the moment, that's enough. Each moment
is all we need, not more.
~Mother Teresa

I Am This Moment

The practice of awareness empowers our lives by focusing our whole attention on being fully present, alert, ready, fearless, able. In the movie *Peaceful Warrior*, an injured gymnast Dan regains his health under the spiritual guidance of a mysterious man whom he calls Socrates. In the final scene, Dan is performing his routine in competition, centering himself by focusing his mind on this imagined dialogue:

Socrates: Where are you?

Dan: Here

Socrates: What time is it?

Dan: Now

Socrates: What are you?

Dan: This moment

Since watching the movie, I have used this little dialogue when I find myself distracted, spinning off in my head. With each question and answer, I am guided back to the present moment, disengaging from the mental gymnastics that scatter my mind in all directions away from here, now. It also eases my grip on my ego identity. I am this moment... and this one. Nothing more, nothing less.

You have probably had the experience of being fully absorbed in an activity. Sometimes awareness happens naturally like that. We can also practice bringing our full attention to the present moment with acceptance, openness, and curiosity. We become one with what is happening. As the saying goes, wherever you are, be there.

Recently, I got a new car that, like my phone, is way too smart for me, but I do like some of the safety features. For example, if I'm drifting out of my lane above a certain speed without using my turn signal, the car assumes that I'm not paying attention. The steering wheel vibrates briefly and a light appears on the dash to alert me. In its own way, the car is reminding me to be here, now, in this moment, mindful of my driving.

We can be grateful for these helpful taps on our mental shoulder. "Hey pal, pay attention. Don't miss your life. This moment is a precious gift, a blessing of infinite grace. Receive it fully, with your whole self. Enter it with openness, gratitude, wonder. It is a miracle."

*Our appointment with life takes place in
the present moment.*
~Thich Nhat Hanh

The Simplicity of Practice

*Life is really simple, but we insist on making
it complicated.*
~Confucius

As we saw in Chapter 1, our soul's longing eventually leads us to the realization that there must be a better way. In this chapter, we've explored the concept of practice, and how practice guides us and permeates our lives as we live this better way. Practice, in essence, is as simple as breathing. We already have everything we need to practice being who we already are.

Like all magnificent things, it's very simple.
~Natalie Babbitt

Everything You Need Is Nothing

Awakening is big business. Pick up any magazine on spirituality and pay attention to the ads. There are retreats, online programs, books, professionals of all kinds, and lots of paraphernalia. It can be overwhelming. But just as you can't learn to ride a bicycle from reading or talking about it, you will never be able to "learn" your way to awakening by taking in more information. You can't think your way to awakening because it isn't a thought.

It is simply our natural state. It is who we are. Its eternal flame is obscured by our efforts, by our thoughts, by our stories. It shines on without regard for our determined quest to find it. The comparison is sometimes made to a fish in the ocean looking for water. But it is even more basic than that. It is like the ocean itself looking for water, unaware of its own nature.

We think awakening is grand, and it is, and at the same time it is quite ordinary. It is not an escape from reality. It *is* reality. Escaping is what we are doing as we search for it, and when we finally exhaust ourselves and stop looking for it, it is revealed. We are revealed.

And what can we do then, but laugh and go on with our day, our ordinary, marvelous, amazing day.

> *Knowing others is wisdom.*
> *Knowing yourself is enlightenment.*
> ~Dao De Jing

Boldly Going Nowhere

Remember the intro to the *Star Trek* series? Their mission was "to boldly go where no one has gone before." I once pulled up behind a car at a stop light and laughed out loud at the bumper sticker: "Boldly going nowhere."

We always think we are, or ought to be, going somewhere, don't we? We might say about a young, talented person, "Mark my words, that young person is going places!" Or we might bemoan our current position. "I am stuck here. I'm not getting anywhere." Our language reflects a belief that staying where we are is not a good thing, that what we want is "just around the corner." Stillness and quietness are not always valued.

In the *Wizard of Oz*, Dorothy sings about a place that she dreams of "over the rainbow." Yet do you remember how the movie ends? When she clicks her heels together and repeats the magic words, "There's no place like home," she finds herself back on the farm and realizes that everything she really wanted had been there all along.

In martial arts class one day, the teacher, who had a third degree black belt in kung fu, reflected that for years he sought to increase his martial arts skills through outer movement: learning more techniques, gaining strength, kicking faster, punching harder, jumping higher. Then he reached a point where the outer activity began to lessen while the inner activity increased. Now, he says, his most powerful martial arts practice is standing meditation. I've heard that, in fact, from more than one martial arts teacher.

Buddhist teacher Pema Chödrön says that one of her favorite sayings is "Sit! Stay! *Heal!*" I get that. Well, first, I'm a dog person, so I think that's funny, having trained many dogs to sit, stay, and *heel*. But I also get it because I've found that when I'm distressed or agitated, when what I most want to do is escape or distract myself in some way, the best thing for me to do is be still and just breathe, not to force quietness, but rather to quit engaging with my mental narrative and allow things to settle gently into quietness.

One time, I was very upset about something someone had done. I fed my anger with judgments and rehearsed how I was going to let this person "have a piece of my mind." That's an interesting saying. Why would I give someone some of my mind? Can I afford to lose any more of it? And if I just change the saying slightly, I am giving someone my "peace" of mind.

When I'm upset, my energy rises into the thoughts in my head. My thoughts get loud! I am restless and definitely not present. I've learned that when I feel like this, I don't try to change my thoughts or force them to calm down. Instead, I turn my attention away from them and just breathe, deeply, quietly, softly. I let my breath lead me back to peace, first in my body, and then in my mind.

I've been fortunate enough in my life to go to many wonderful places and to do many adventurous things, but sometimes the wisest course is to go nowhere and do nothing. And that is indeed bold.

Without going outside, you may know the whole world
Without looking through the window,
you may see the ways of heaven
The farther you go, the less you know
Thus the sage knows without traveling
He sees without looking
He succeeds without doing
~Dao De Jing

There Is No How

Do or do not. There is no try.
~Yoda

If, as Yoda says, there is no try, then how does awakening happen? How do I get it? Where are the instructions? If I read this book, practice these techniques, listen to this podcast, attend this workshop, devote myself to this teacher, read another book, breathe a certain way, think a certain way, meditate a certain way, chant a mantra, go to a retreat, read another book—will I achieve my goal? Will I pass the test and get my certificate? Will I be enlightened then?

How do I do this? Just tell me how. Please.

You want the secret? Okay, here it is. There is no how. Take it from one who has tried everything listed above. And more.

But then how ...

There is no how. There is no way to get from here to there, because there is no there. There is no journey because there is nowhere to go. There is no technique, because there is nothing to do. There is no way of teaching because there is nothing to learn.

The brain can't grasp this. Literally, the brain can't understand this, because our brains think. That's what they do. Sometimes they do it really well. But you cannot think your way to enlightenment. Because enlightenment transcends thought. In fact, enlightenment doesn't exist.

What?

Well, it doesn't exist in the sense of a static state. It is dynamic, offering an opportunity in every moment to enter the holy instant, as *A Course in Miracles* calls it. The holy instant reveals all eternity to us in the perfect bliss of oneness.

Did you miss the holy instant in this moment? That's okay. Here is another moment. And another.

I'm trying, but...

Don't try.

Then how...

Just allow. Take a deep breath and surrender. Your breath will teach you everything. You don't have to think to breathe. You just have to not interfere. Allow your body to show you how to be fully present in this moment. Instead of "taking" a few deep breaths, just be present as a witness as your body opens and receives the gift of breath. It knows just what to do. Let go of everything. It only takes a moment. Because a moment is all there is.

Surrender is the name of the spiritual game.
~Adyashanti

Embracing Yin in a Yang World

You are probably familiar with the yin/yang symbol, a circle divided in half with a curved line, one side black, representing yin, and the other white, representing yang. The circle represents the oneness of duality, and helps us understand the relationship of apparent opposites, existing only in balanced relativity with each other.

Our western culture highly values yang energy. Yang energy is active, hot, rising, powerful. When someone is wildly successful, driving forward, moving up, dominating the competition, unstoppable, we might say, "Wow, she's on fire!" Some familiar sayings also reflect this preference: idle hands do the devil's work, make the most of every minute, increase productivity, we can rest when we're dead, time is money, move up or move out.

There is nothing inherently wrong with yang energy. On the contrary, as the manifesting energy of creation, it is a necessary and natural aspect of life's rhythm and harmony. But it requires balance and is complemented by yin energy. Yin is still, receptive, dark, nurturing. It is the womb from which creation emerges. It is the fertile earth, the energy of gathering, returning to the source, the energy of harvest. Following the yang season of summer, yin's season is fall, moving from the expansion of summer's growth to the quiet, restorative rest of winter.

In recent years, many areas of the world have experienced record heat and drought. Rivers and lakes are drying up and wildfires are racing across the land. We sometimes describe such fires as "raging." I can't help but wonder if these fires in particular, and global warming in general, are reflections back to us of the imbalance we have created by such devoted allegiance to yang energy. Perhaps it's no coincidence that the yin organ of autumn is the lungs, the organ most directly vulnerable to fire and smoke.

What does this reveal to us about our inner imbalance, our raging fires of hostility and division, our willingness to destroy, our consuming devastation, fed by anger, and underneath the anger, fear? Nature seeks balance. Our spirits seek balance. Our prolonged elevation of yang qualities suggests a need for turning to and embracing yin. As we become still and turn inward, yin energy welcomes us, nurtures us, and encourages us to rest, to contemplate, to listen, to receive. Yin is the energy of being rather than doing.

The *Dao De Jing* teaches that strong winds can't last forever and violent storms exhaust themselves. We drain our energy without replenishment when we expend our inner reserves ever striving, ever doing, ever in conflict with ourselves and each other. Our bodies become ill. Our emotions are in turmoil.

Our spirits, like nature, will find balance one way or another. We need not force it. We can simply allow it. When we are feeling overwhelmed by yang energy, when we are overdoing, angry, exhausted, we can take a few moments to relax, to simplify, to breathe, to be still, to be replenished by the earth's nurturing yin energy.

> *Outer world is just the mirror image*
> *of your inner world.*
> ~Amit Ray

Practice Becomes the Way We Live

What you practice is what you manifest.
~Fay Weldon

We are always "practicing" something because we are always manifesting something. This is the nature of existence. We have conscious practices that we set time aside for, and we have our default practices that run a background program that generates our perspective and our way of engaging with ourselves and the world around us. The intention of conscious practice is to gradually modify our default program until the two merge and run in harmony. At that point, our conscious practice simply reminds us of, and reinforces, our internal alignment in such a way that our life unfolds naturally and effortlessly. We manifest the union that we experience with all creation and the source of all creation. We breathe love.

*I practice martial arts not to win over other people
but to win over my own heart.*
~Tony Jaa

We Learn by Doing

*For the things we have to learn before we can do them,
we learn by doing them.*
~Aristotle

We weave practice into our lives as we go through our day. We practice to enable us to apply what we learn in the rest of our lives. This is especially so when we find ourselves hooked, churned up, thrown off balance. Sometimes we have attached ourselves to a narrative and are poised to react to our story rather than to respond to what is, or grief presses all the air out of our lungs until we can't breathe, or we are hurt and we want to lash out in pain, or fear has clamped our minds shut and we seek desperately to escape.

All those descriptions apply to me at various times. Sometimes I'm teetering on the razor's edge, and sometimes I have fallen off. This is part of practice too. But we don't only practice when times are tough. Practicing when the sun is shining is what sustains us during the inevitable storms of life. Whatever your specific practice is that sustains you and restores you to inner balance—praying, meditating, exercising, gardening, cooking, reading, or as a friend said, napping—is less important than just doing it.

As noted before, the best practice is the one you'll actually do. So quit measuring yourself against someone else's standard. Listen within and find what makes your soul sing in your body, and do that. And remember that our most important practice is simply loving ourselves just the way we are.

Love yourself first and everything else falls into line.
~Lucille Ball

Invest in Loss

Take chances, make mistakes. That's how you grow.
~Mary Tyler Moore

Invest in loss? That does not sound like wise financial planning or a promising career strategy. Yet it is a slogan we practice with in martial arts, passed down by tai chi master Cheng

Man Ching. In the martial arts context, it means being willing to lose in order to gain skill and knowledge and ultimately mastery.

For example, I used to spar with a student who was consistently able to move past my defenses with a particular move. Because I embraced the principle of investing in loss, I always asked to spar with him, and I always asked him to use that move. Then one day, I suddenly countered the move successfully. We were both surprised! He gave me a high five and there was much laughter and celebration. Almost without knowing it, all that time I was gathering information, experimenting with different responses, and learning what didn't work. We had worked in concert rather than in opposition. And when the moment was right, success simply happened.

There is so much we can learn when we are not attached to "winning." I find that this principle has begun to permeate my life, sometimes with surprising results. When I am not afraid to "lose," I can pay attention to what is happening and respond appropriately. An argument becomes a conversation. A verbal attack is deflected with compassion. A misunderstanding offers an opportunity to listen.

We've probably heard the saying "The best defense is a good offense." Perhaps the best defense is no offense…and no defense either.

> *If nothing within you stays rigid, outward things will disclose themselves. Moving, be like water. Still, be like a mirror. Respond like an echo.*
> ~Bruce Lee

When Practice Throws You a Surprise Party

When you least expect it, your practice will reveal itself. Once, while walking along a forest trail with a friend and our dogs, we came to a narrow plank laid down to make a bridge over a creek. As I started to walk across, her big dog decided that she wanted to be in front of me. Before my friend could warn me, her dog came running up behind me and, in racing to get past, slammed into my left leg, knocking it upwards and spinning me sideways on the plank.

By all reason, I should have ended up in the creek. But somehow I didn't fall. As I spun, I managed to maintain my equilibrium, turning on my axis, and ended up facing sideways on the plank, perfectly balanced in a standing pose often practiced in martial arts. Poised there as my mind took in the dog running ahead on the trail, I felt sort of foolish and amazed at the same time. I slowly turned to look at my friend and said, "I have no idea how I did that."

Perhaps that is not entirely true. My martial arts practice involves a lot of balance and responding to the unexpected. When the dog bumped me, my body just did what it is trained to do. I really had little to do with it in terms of analyzing the situation, making a plan, and executing it. It was over before my mind caught up and figured out what had happened. Reflecting on it later, I understood that this is why we practice. We practice so that when needed, our training kicks in and operates without much conscious supervision. We internalize our practice and it becomes part of who we are.

We are always practicing something. I got to wondering what else I'm practicing. Am I practicing kindness or meanness? Compassion or judgment? Forgiveness or anger? Generosity or withholding? Connection or separation? Faith or fear? We practice intentionally and consciously what we want to manifest spontaneously when something catches us off guard, so that our training will activate when needed, guiding us as we engage with others and the world around us.

I'm going to pay more attention to what I'm practicing as I go through my day. For one thing, I want to practice not taking things personally. I could also use some brushing up on taking responsibility for my own feelings. I would like to practice taking the long view when considering my response to something in the moment. And I definitely need to fluff and buff my practice of maintaining good boundaries.

The incident at the creek taught me that what I practice consciously will become my automatic response in unguarded moments.

> *An ounce of practice is generally worth more*
> *than a ton of theory.*
> ~E. F. Schumacher

Carried by Practice

Our practice not only helps us in responding, but it also protects us and sustains us when we don't have the energy to try. One day I was caught up in a spiritual tantrum. A friend patiently listened to me rant about my frustration:

> *I'm not feeling very kumbaya. I don't want to cultivate compassion or acceptance. I feel judgmental and angry. I don't like people very much right now. I'm mad at the Universe for its relentless offering of opportunities to practice in my personal life, my family's life, friends' lives, and I don't even know what to do with all the global angst and suffering. I am tired of practicing. Practice, practice, practice. I'm done.*

After giving voice to my meltdown, I didn't feel better. I felt worse. After releasing all that pent up churning, I went home and plummeted into crushing despair. I sank into surrendered silence. Breathe. One breath. Another.

Then Practice spoke to me:

That's okay. You don't need to practice right now. Stop struggling. You are wearing yourself out needlessly. I will carry you. I will get you through this.

I realized practice is not a discipline. It's a relationship. A healthy relationship of give and take on both sides. A relationship of trust and familiarity. And love. The deeper I go with my practice and the more consistent I am, the more I learn to trust that in tough times practice sustains me. As promised, it does carry me and get me through. I had forgotten that practice is not a burden; it's a friend.

> *Behind the hardness there is fear*
> *And if you touch the heart of the fear*
> *You find sadness*
> *And if you touch the sadness*
> *You find the vast blue sky*
> ~Rick Fields

Now Is the Time

> *Each day*
> *Is one day less to live*
> *Do not waste it*
> *So that when death comes*

I often emphasize and encourage practice. I talk about the "razor's edge" of practice, that place where we are challenged to release, expand, embrace, accept, forgive. The place where we meet fear on the battlefield and bow in respect. The place where we experience the distress of not knowing. The place where we come face to face with reality and find that it looks just…like…us. Not the us that we tell ourselves about, not the us that we hide from others, not the us that we want others to see—no, the us as we are, just as we are, right now in this moment.

How do we practice when, well, when things are like they are? How do we practice when everything from viruses to earthquakes to politics to wars to not enough toilet paper threatens our equanimity? When our routines are disrupted, our expectations disregarded, our assumptions revealed and proven false? When fear runs rampant in our minds, and our hearts are shattered in grief?

This is precisely the time to practice, to practice, as Pema Chödrön says, like our hair is on fire. (That always makes me laugh…and motivates me!) This is when the practice we do when things are easy shows up to support us and sustain us when things are hard. This is when the trust we have built up in our practice is put to the test and carries us steady on the course.

And what is it exactly that we are practicing? What we can. Allowing. Awareness. Loving kindness. Meditation. Too much? That's okay. Practice mindful breathing. Start with this breath. Now this one. It is enough.

The point is not to add more to our to do lists, or to reach some self-imposed standard, and certainly not some other-imposed standard, but to permeate our lives with compassion, beginning with ourselves. How many times have I heard someone say, "I have to," or "I should have," or some version of self-demand or self-failure. When I hear this, I just want to say, "It's okay. We are all muddling through as best we can, learning and adapting as we go."

Bring awareness and compassion to the muddling. It is enough.

Now is the time, not to be perfect, not to know everything. Now is the time to practice, to practice being here, now. Now is the time to practice remembering who we are, always safe and ever loved.

Practice remembering one breath at a time. It is enough.

"When every breath
Becomes a prayer
When every step
Becomes a meditation
When every word
Becomes a song of love
When every heartbeat
Pulses gratitude
Then…" he paused
"Then what?" they urged
He smiled and bowed

PART 3

LIVING AN AWAKENED LIFE

CHAPTER 5

Showered with Grace

*For he maketh his sun to rise on the evil and on the
good, and sendeth rain on the just and on the unjust.*
~Matthew 5:45

Our eternal practice ultimately leads us to compassion, described in the *Dao De Jing* as abiding in tenderness. We can think of compassion as another one of our eternal practices, and it is. But to me, compassion is also a gift, a gift generously bestowed on us in the form of grace, grace that waters us like the rain, warms us like the sunshine, and embraces us with infinite love. It is a gift that naturally arises within, and spills out from, the awakened heart.

*Those who long for love
Look for someone to give it to them
Not realizing they are showered with love
From the soul of every person
From the rocks on the mountain
From each star in the heavens
From the tiny violet beside the path*

Allowing Ourselves to Be Loved

*The journey from teaching about love to allowing
myself to be loved proved much longer than I realised.*
~Henri Nouwen

We sometimes think acceptance of reality means not struggling against something that we don't like. But we overlook the one area where at least some of us are the most resistant to accepting. Why are we so reluctant to believe that we are loved, that we are lovable, that we *are* the expression of Love in form?

While we are so busy bestowing our gracious acceptance on everything around us, we draw the line at accepting for ourselves the generous blessing of infinite and unconditional love that breathes us to life with every breath. We embrace the concept that we should love others, even our enemies. But we deny ourselves that same love unless we believe that we deserve it, unless somehow we have earned the gift that is already ours, that has always been ours since the first stirring of creation.

When a fellow blogger wrote, "Who am I to be enlightened?" I replied, "Who are you *not* to be enlightened?" Enlightenment is our natural state, in harmony with the music of creation, joined in sacred union with all that is and with the source of all that is. Wisdom teachings from all traditions assure us that we are beloved children of the Universe, created in the image of the divine, wholly lovable just as we are, and unconditionally loved without exception.

Feel the hands of God cupping your face, see God's smiling eyes looking into yours, and listen as God tells you how perfect you are, how cherished you are, how brilliantly your spirit shines. Allow yourself to receive the birthright of your existence. Allow the flame of the Beloved to ignite your soul and blaze forth for all to see. This is the greatest gift you can give to anyone.

Desperado
Why don't you come to your senses?
Come down from your fences
Open the gate

Breaking the Crust of Fear

Sometimes a storm roars through your life
A sudden wind whipping, lightning flashing, thunder
crashing, rain gushing, heart thumping storm
Leaving you breathless
And more alive than you have ever been
Snapping, sizzling, sparking
Like lightning hit and lit you up
You look out and see
The world is new

It's hard for us to receive this gift of grace when our hearts are closed. I once went to see an energy healer. During my appointment, he started thumping rhythmically on my chest, alternating hands. At first the thumps were gentle, but gradually he increased the intensity until my whole body became a drum. The thumping became so powerful that I felt like my chest would crack open and my heart would explode. I tried to stay calm, but I confess I was relieved when he stopped.

Echoes of the thumping reverberated in my body as I started in with questions about what had happened. Reluctant to verbally debrief a session, he finally responded to my pestering by simply saying that there was a crust around my heart and he broke it off.

Although I paid to have my heart liberated that time, I've found that life will often do it for free. A family member disappoints us, a friend betrays us, we lose someone dear, a love is not returned, our feelings get hurt, a child is struggling. Life offers us opportunities every day to make a choice: to guard our hearts behind thick, crusty walls, or to open the door to the pain that enters hand in hand with joy. Yes, hand in hand. That's why sometimes we cry with joy and sometimes laugh through our tears.

Parenting is sometimes described as walking around with your heart outside of your body. I remember years of repressing the grief I felt over having an autistic child, until the love buried alongside the pain broke through the concrete like an irrepressible sprout. The love bloomed bright red, the color of a bleeding heart. The pain was scary. It hurt. But when I pushed it away, it festered deep. Eventually, I learned to cradle my pain with love, to hold it gently and soothe it with compassion. When we lean into the pain, a whole world of beauty opens up. The love and the pain—both exquisite.

What is it about love that calls us to its stony shore like the Sirens of mythology? I think it's because we recognize that shore as home. Love is our natural state, the birthplace of our soul. Our life's journey is one of returning home. And like the ships that heeded the Sirens' call and crashed upon the rocks, our homecoming will break apart the shell around our hearts, and set us free once more.

A heart that breaks open can contain
the whole universe.
~Joanna Macy

The Gift of Receiving

*Until we can receive with an open heart, we are never
really giving with an open heart.*
~Brené Brown

We can't hear love's call if we are not willing to receive its
blessing. On occasion, I have heard someone express hesitation to participate in a get-together because, as they said, they
felt that they had nothing of value to offer that particular day.
Maybe they were worried about something, or distracted, or
just in a slump. They really wanted to go, but thought that
they should not because they believed they had nothing to
give.

What a lot of pressure we put on ourselves. First, that is
a big assumption about not having anything of value to offer.
Our very presence can be a gift that we are not even aware
of giving. Second, I was struck by the idea that it's not okay
to just receive. Maybe on a particular day we need support,
we need caring, we need to be held in the energy of acceptance just the way we are. Can we give ourselves permission
to receive what we need without the pressure to generate a
profound thought, a wise suggestion, or a funny observation?

Balance sheets work with money, but not always with life.
How we assess life value is often arbitrary and subjective,
reflecting much more about self-judgment than about some
objective measurement. We often measure our value by some
outward manifestation of giving, seeing everything else as
being in the red debit column. We misunderstand or overlook
the value of being fully who we are.

On the days when, in our own estimation, we have nothing
to offer, if we can give ourselves permission to show up as we
are, to receive caring from others, we offer to others a model

of self-awareness and self-acceptance. We teach others how to receive caring and support and understanding.

Your greatest value is not in always being "on" or in giving something to others. Your greatest value is in being fully who you are, without pretense, without judgment. You are precious beyond measure by virtue of your very existence. True relationship, true connection, is an exchange of energy. When you allow yourself to receive, you offer someone else the blessing of giving. When we let others see us as we are, we give them permission to be who they are.

So please be generous with the gift of being yourself, including allowing yourself to receive when you are in need. And on the balance sheet of life, that is priceless.

> *When we give cheerfully and accept gratefully,*
> *everyone is blessed.*
> ~Maya Angelou

We All Need a Village

> *The simple act of caring is heroic.*
> ~Edward Albert

Most of us have heard the saying that it takes a village to raise a child. However, I'm pretty sure that all of us need a village, maybe not to raise each other, but to care for each other. Sometimes the Universe showers us with grace through the kindness of others. Here are a couple of examples. I bet you can think of your own.

Several years ago, I was going through an especially challenging time. So when a neighbor, who knew some of what I was experiencing, asked how I was doing, I responded that

I was having a hard time, and that I needed something sweet and sugary (how enlightened). Later when I stopped by her house, her counter was covered with ingredients. She said she was making cookies.

"Were you making them anyway, or because I said I wanted something sweet?" I asked.

"I am making them for you," she answered matter-of-factly.

At which point I burst into tears.

I was surprised by how much I needed someone to care about me. That simple gesture of baking cookies crashed into my heart with compassion. My heart broke open with overwhelming gratitude. I felt seen and loved.

In the second example, I realized that compassion is sometimes a team sport.

The beginning of this story is that my zippered wallet containing my money, credit cards, driver's license, and phone fell out of my jacket pocket onto the street as I got in my car and drove off. The end of the story is that I got it all back. But it's the middle of the story that matters here.

At least seven people, all strangers to me, all busy with their lives, chose to play a part in getting my wallet with all its contents back to me. Amazing, and then again, it isn't, because I was reminded that many people, given the chance, will choose to be kind. At some level, we recognize our interconnectedness and our shared humanity. Jesus noted that whatever we do to others, we do *to him*. He didn't say it was *as if* we did it to him. He said exactly what he meant.

Life is short, and we have but little time to gladden
the hearts of those who travel this way with us. Oh, be
swift to love. Make haste to be kind.
~Henri-Frédéric Amiel

Compassion Begins at Home

One time I accidentally caused an injury to my dog. I felt horrible and raced her to the vet, who assured me that my dog would be fine, that we all make mistakes, and that I was a good "dog mother" for bringing her in so quickly. Despite her kindness, I was crying and arguing that I was a terrible person who, through my own thoughtlessness, had hurt this innocent little animal. I was mired in self-condemnation, and it didn't help that my dog was licking my hand and wagging her tail, trying to make me feel better.

The love we long for, the peace we pray for, the compassion we hunger for, all bubble up from the spring of self-acceptance. It is sometimes so hard to love ourselves, especially when in our own eyes we have fallen short. Wouldn't it be wonderful if we could love ourselves the way our dogs love us?

> *Walk sweetly with yourself. Find every reason*
> *possible to love who you are.*
> ~Emmanuel's Book II

Prescription: Compassion for Self

> *You've been criticizing yourself for years and it hasn't*
> *worked. Try approving of yourself and see what happens.*
> ~Louise L. Hay

Compassion for ourselves can even be medically prescribed! During a visit to my naturopath, she made some suggestions for diet changes and supplements. She wrote down her instructions and handed me the page.

When I got home, I reviewed her list of instructions. The last item said:

I laughed out loud. What kind of prescription was this? What sort of doctor does this, I asked myself.

Apparently a doctor who cares about her whole patient, who wants her patient to be whole, to feel whole. A doctor who knows that without compassion, all the supplements in the world will still leave her patient lacking. Unless the patient can open her heart to her own self, then all the doctor's care will be for naught.

How many millions of dollars are spent every year on self-improvement? What violence do we do to ourselves by judging ourselves as always falling short, never being good enough as we are? At times, we speak of ourselves with such self-criticism, such disappointment, such hatred. Condemning ourselves to eternal inadequacy, we desperately search for some external answer to our distress, for someone to tell us what to do.

So here is the answer, right on the prescription paper—compassion for self. Just for one moment, take a deep breath, drop all the judgment, and give yourself a smile. Doctor's orders.

> *Give yourself the love you're willing to give to others.*
> ~Mahin Ismail

Calling for Love

> *What is the difference between an enlightened person and an unenlightened person? The unenlightened person sees a difference.*
> ~Miracles Magazine

At a time when the divisions in the world seem wider than ever, I sometimes struggle to find our commonality of enlightenment. Occasionally people ask me how I cope with it all. They want to know how I find compassion for people saying and doing things that, at least to some, seem incomprehensibly terrible.

The short answer is that I do better at some times than at other times.

Many studies show that our well-being is directly related to the connection we have with others, and we are only connected to others when our hearts are open. But let's face it, there are plenty of folks out there I really don't want to be connected to. So how do I maintain an open heart?

A Course in Miracles teaches that love has no opposite. Love is all there is. (Wasn't that the title of a Beatles song? No, that was "Love is all you need." Also true.) When something happens that blocks our awareness of love's infinite and eternal presence, we experience that separation as fear. When we feel afraid, we reflect our sense of separation from others through negative thoughts, words, and behavior. In reality, what we are doing is seeking reconnection. We are calling for love.

Does this mean that I shrug at discrimination and persecution? Do I ignore the devastation we cause to our earth home? Do I turn away from the horrors of war? Do I pretend that everything is always pleasant? No, of course not.

Everything we do or say or think is either an expression of love (when we experience connection) or a call for love (when we mistakenly believe we are separated). Everything is one or the other. Everything. It's that simple.

When I can remember this, I find that it is much easier to keep my heart open. When I look out at the world of suffering, manifested in so many ways, I feel sadness, tenderness, compassion for all the pain. I feel the pain of people striking out in anger, the pain of the hungry and oppressed, the pain of violence and cruelty, the pain of desperation, the pain of addiction, the pain of power grabbing, the pain of divisiveness, the pain of all the ways that we separate ourselves from each other, from all of nature, from our planet.

We can stand for justice while recognizing our common humanity, we can sense the pain and fear underneath acts of unspeakable cruelty as we reach out to protect and comfort the injured, because we understand deep down that peace will not flow from a heart closed to those we deem "other." And when our own hearts do close in pain and fear, we can extend our embrace of compassion to include ourselves.

We can practice in little ways so that we can cope with the big stuff. Next time someone is unkind to me, instead of reacting defensively, I can take a deep breath and think, "Dude, you are seriously calling for love." Someone cuts me off in traffic? "Hey, I see you are needing some love over there." I know that sounds trivial in the context of world events, but big hurts and little affronts are all the same. If it isn't an expression of love, it's a call for love.

I don't have to agree with everyone, or even like everyone. I just need to recognize that the spark of universal energy that shines in me does indeed shine in all of us. Just the way we are. Compassion is not just for some of us; it's for all of us. Everyone. Even me.

A friend once posed the question: Are we our brother's keeper? Yes, I replied, because we *are* our brother.

We are here to awaken from our illusion
of separateness.
~Thich Nhat Hanh

The Trap of Being "Good"

We want so much to be good and to be seen as good. I want to be a good person, a good mother, a good friend, and so on. I want others to see me as good. I want my goodness reflected back to me in how others think of me, talk about me, and act towards me.

This seems like a desirable aspiration. So we strive to do better and be better. This striving is like holding an umbrella up that keeps us dry when grace is showering down all around us. We forget that grace is naturally flowing over us, within us, and through us. Water does not strive. Grace does not strive. Goodness is our natural state. Seeking to conform ourselves with some self-imposed standard of goodness is a trap, preventing us from experiencing and expressing our natural grace-filled goodness.

Being "good" can also result in avoidance of thoughts or behaviors that do not meet this ideal of goodness. We might become defensive instead of receptive when someone reflects back to us something we've done or said that falls short. We rationalize, justify, explain—whatever it takes to deflect an honest assessment or genuine listening.

Or perhaps we go to the opposite extreme. If we acknowledge our imperfections, our identity as a good person is crushed, and we are lost in self-judgment and condemnation. If I do something bad, then I must not be good. Within this mindset of duality, I am one or the other.

We can be so invested in our identity of goodness, and fearful of not measuring up in our own eyes or the eyes of others, that we cannot accept ourselves as complex human beings with a full range of thoughts and behaviors. We lose any chance of being or knowing who we are, and with that loss, any chance of true connection with others. It's like "my people will talk to your people," but it's really "my facade of goodness will interface with your facade of goodness."

This issue of being a good person comes up a lot in conversations about bias, especially about unconscious or implicit bias. Bias is often denied because someone is deemed to be a "good person" and therefore cannot be biased, because any bias would make the person "bad." That denial then effectively closes off any open dialogue or genuine self-reflection about the inevitable existence of biases woven into our conscious and unconscious thoughts and behaviors.

Such denial also takes a lot of effort to maintain. It is exhausting to fragment ourselves, defending the parts that reinforce our goodness, and rejecting or hiding the parts that don't. Perhaps we can take a lesson from one of my favorite children's books, *The Fire Cat*, by Esther Averill:

Pickles, you are not a bad cat. You are not a good cat. You are good and bad. And bad and good. You are a mixed-up cat.

Our resistance to open and honest self-acceptance doesn't make us better people. Instead, it strengthens those aspects of ourselves we try to keep hidden. As the saying goes, what we resist, persists. However, when brought to the light of acknowledgment with honesty and compassion, those parts locked up in the darkness can be transformed with the love of understanding and forgiveness.

It's not as scary as it sounds. On the contrary, it is a relief. Not long ago, someone reflected back to me something I had done that was hurtful. At one time, I would have gotten defensive and explained how the person had misinterpreted what had happened. My "goodness" would be reaffirmed. I admit, that impulse was still there for a moment. But I was able to take a deep breath and listen. That listening helped me see the situation from the other person's perspective, to acknowledge the pain they had experienced. While I couldn't go back and change what I had done, I could accept responsibility for my own words and actions. I could accept this person's experience without trying to invalidate it or fix it. Instead, I could learn from it. I could consider how I might have handled things differently, and how I might be able to take that awareness with me into future interactions.

Goodness is not the issue. I was not a bad person because I had done something hurtful. I was not a good person because I listened. Honesty is the issue. Compassion is the issue—compassion for the other person's pain, and compassion for myself as a person who makes mistakes.

When we release ourselves from the trap of goodness, we are free. And in that freedom, genuine relationship is possible. And that is good.

I am larger, better than I thought; I did not know
I held so much goodness.
~Walt Whitman

A Touch of Compassion

Touch
Touch this
This too
Touch everything that comes within your reach
Touch it with compassion
Touch it gently
With the vastness of your being
Touch it sweetly
With the love that sings your soul

When we release ourselves from the trap of being good, we discover that compassion extends beyond ourselves and others, to connect us to everything, absolutely everything, within and without. We stay "in touch" with all of creation.

We think of touch as an external, physical connection. But touch can also be internal, emotional, energetic. We can touch with the heart of compassion. Absolutely anything that arises in our field of awareness can be touched with compassion.

This is easy when we are naturally drawn to an experience that "touches" our heart. When we see a child in distress, a friend in need, an animal suffering, we instinctively reach out to comfort, to soothe, to support. But what happens when something does not attract our sympathy, when something arises that we draw away from with judgment or fear?

I can feel compassion for a server or cashier facing a rude customer. But can I feel compassion for the person who is being rude? Perhaps. How about someone who is mean to me or to someone I love? Harder. What if I am watching something on the news that leaves me in despair or sparks outrage? Sometimes impossible. What do I do when compassion is not forthcoming?

I touch my resistance with compassion. I touch my condemnation of others with compassion. Maybe I judge myself for my compassion fail. Touch that judgment with compassion.

Our own hurt places, our shame, our insecurities, our painful memories, our regrets, our embarrassment, our self-criticism, our anxieties and fears—yes, all these can be touched with compassion. Whatever arises in our thoughts or experience is what is calling to us for acknowledgment, acceptance, compassion. And if we are unable to feel any compassion for these dark places? If we are unable to even look at them, much less touch them? Yes, you are catching on. Touch that inability with compassion.

Touch connects, softens, comforts, heals, and opens. It opens us to the next layer that asks for compassion. And the next. Until compassion pours forth like the gentle rain that falls on everything without regard to merit. Nourishing, cleansing, spurring growth and beauty.

Compassion is revolution.
~bumper sticker

Failing Better

Fail. Fail again. Fail better.
~Samuel Beckett,
quoted by Pema Chödrön as the title of her book

We might understand the concept of touching everything with compassion, but sometimes we just don't do it. We fail. We fail again. And sometimes forgiving ourselves just seems too hard. I mentioned earlier that my model for forgiveness was my dog, who licked my hand to soothe my distress after I inadvertently caused her injury. When a dog is not handy, we need to find other ways to forgive ourselves when we fall short.

We don't like to experience failure. We don't even like to think about it. So we deny it, reframe it, avoid it, hide it, anything to not face it and feel the pain. The pain of not facing failure becomes shame. We beat ourselves up with I should haves, I shouldn't haves, if onlys. We tell ourselves stories with different outcomes. We pretend. And in the process, we lose who we really are. Then we can't truly connect with others, leaving us feeling alone and afraid.

I've found that the more I deny my failures, the more I repeat them. Have you ever tried to unwrap something sealed with that cellophane that sticks to your fingers? You try to throw it away, but it's still there. You fling your hand towards the trash and think you are rid of it only to see that it jumped to another finger and it's still there. Like clinging cellophane, some failures are annoying. But others live deep in the dungeons of our soul. The failures that haunt me the most are the ones where I let someone down, or let myself down, when I wasn't the best person I could be. This is especially true where my children are concerned. Is there a parent out there who doesn't cringe at the memory of some way that they failed their children? There are still things that I have a hard time admitting.

But over time, I began to accept or to at least acknowledge some of the ways I have failed. I've even admitted a few of my shortcomings to others. Lo and behold, instead of shock and rejection, I discovered I was in good company.

I'm a little more gentle with myself these days. They say charity begins at home. When I can find compassion for myself, it's easier to find it for others. Once, when I was frustrated with my son's autistic behavior, someone said, "Perhaps he's doing the best he can." She was right. He was. Perhaps we all are doing the best we can. We will have successes and failures. And the failures will sometimes hurt. We might not be able to avoid failure, but with some compassion, forgiveness, and patience, we can fail better. Life will undoubtedly offer us many opportunities to practice!

We cling
With such sweet believing
To our suffering
And call it brave

Until finally
There is nothing left
Sinking in surrender
Only then
Is grace

The Grandson Chronicles

The greatest wisdom often comes from the smallest people. Here are a few of my favorite grandson stories that taught me about being showered, and showering others, with the grace of compassion.

Feed Me and Love Me

My grandson was getting into a little trouble for acting up at school. As I chatted with him about his behavior, he came up with his own plan for trying to do better. It was a good plan. When I asked him how we could help him and support him in implementing his plan, he thought for a moment and then replied,

"Feed me and love me."

Isn't this what we all need for help and support? To be fed with patience, encouragement, friendship, honesty, mercy, listening, appreciation, attention. Yes, and sometimes with real food. To be loved with compassion, acceptance, delight, non-judgment, and without conditions.

I had sat down with my grandson intending to offer him guidance, but instead he taught me. I bowed to my young wisdom teacher and thanked him for this lesson.

And a little child shall lead them.
~Isaiah 11:6

George Is Fine the Way He Is

My grandson came home from a shopping trip with his mom, eager to show me his new stuffed animal, a great find from Goodwill. He called it a monkey, but we soon established that it was a lemur. He named it George.

Further inquiry led to Internet searches and an entertaining and informative documentary about lemurs. Watching the beautifully filmed documentary, I noticed that all the lemurs had something that George did not—a tail. I examined George and discovered a little ripped place on his backside where at one time a tail was undoubtedly attached.

Instead of pointing this out, I went to the store the next day and bought what I would need to create a new tail for George. I thought my grandson would be pleased when I showed him that George had lost his tail and that I could make him a new one. However, after considering this for hardly a moment, my grandson hugged George close and said, "That's okay, Nana. George is fine the way he is."

As I took a minute to let that sink in, away went George the tailless lemur, bouncing happily in my grandson's arms as they ran off to play.

> *To be fully seen by somebody and be loved*
> *anyhow—this is a human offering that can*
> *border on miraculous.*
> ~Elizabeth Gilbert

Feeling Loved

When my phone rang one morning, the caller ID showed my daughter's name. Thinking it was her, I answered with a "Good morning, sweetie."

But the caller was my grandson, who exclaimed, "Nana, how did you know it was me?!"

"I just knew," I fibbed.

Even though my usual nickname for him is Honey Bunny, he responded to the generic "sweetie" term of endearment with the assumption that it was meant for him. How marvelous.

When he was a baby, I made up a song for him to the tune of *Jesus Loves Me*. I would sing the song over and over, each time substituting the name of someone who loved him. For example:

[Nana] loves me
This I know
Because she always tells me so
She loves me more than the stars above
I am blessed to be so loved
Yes, [Nana] loves me
Yes, [Nana] loves me
Yes, [Nana] loves me
She always tells me so

As he got older, I would start the ritual with the question "Who loves you?" He would name someone. After the first verse, I would ask "Who else loves you?" And so on. To my delight, he would often name himself as someone who loved him.

His quick and unquestioning assumption that morning that "sweetie" referred to him tells me that somehow, in his childhood world of scary things that go bump in the night, despite all the mistakes that we make as parents and grandparents, he has absorbed the certainty that he is loved.

May we all feel so cherished.

Someone Who Cares

My grandson called me one night. He was crying so hard I could not understand the words he gasped through his sobs. I thought something horrible had happened. Trying to stay calm as I was searching for my car keys to race over there, I asked him again and again to tell me what happened. Finally I heard:

"Mom ... put ... lettuce ... on ... my ... taco," he wailed.

Um, really?

My anxiety melted into relief, and maybe a bit of chagrin at what I saw as an over the top reaction.

"I ... just ... wanted ... to ... talk ... to ... someone ... who ... cares."

It wasn't really about the lettuce at all. His mother loves him very much of course, but at that moment she was the perpetrator of the taco debacle, so he sought solace from someone he thought he could count on to care. He wanted what we all want, to be heard and to feel unconditionally loved.

We sometimes judge someone's distress as worthy or unworthy of our caring. We get so distracted by the circumstances that we miss the underlying need for emotional touch. *A Course in Miracles* teaches that we are never upset for the reason we think. So next time we are upset, or faced with someone else who is, we might pause and look beneath the situation for what need is really being expressed, whether our own or someone else's. And that is usually going to be a need for compassion.

How thankful I was that I had not spoken the teasing remark that had been on the tip of my tongue. Instead, I offered a listening heart with an abundance of compassion poured out over his hurting soul. Satisfied, he calmed down and we said our goodbyes. I don't know what happened with the taco, but he had been fed with what really mattered.

Love—asked for, given, received. An eternal exchange of an infinite commodity. Like breathing. Inhaling and exhaling endless compassion.

> *My bounty is as boundless as the sea, my love as deep.*
> *The more I give to thee, the more I have,*
> *for both are infinite.*
> ~William Shakespeare, *Romeo and Juliet*

I Love You "Morst"

My grandson and I have always had a special bond. We often try to outdo each other in expressing our affection. He called one night to tell me about his day. The end of our conversation went like this:

Me: Goodnight, Honey Bunny. I love you.

Him: I love you more.

Me: I love you most.

Him: (after a pause) Well…I love you MORST!

He won that round. Such a simple little conversation, but we both ended the call feeling loved and cherished. Even now, as I write these words, my heart still smiles.

Just a few words, but what a lasting impact. The words we speak carry such power to embrace, or harm. If we could only stop to think about what effect our words leave in their wake, we might choose our words more carefully.

Words are cheap
But can cost dear
Take care with what you speak
Let love guide your tongue
And only blessings fall from your lips

At Least There's No Volcano

My grandson, who can sometimes be a glass-half-empty kind of kid, told me one day that he had decided to look on the brighter side of life.

"Yep," he said, "if I'm feeling bad, I can just look out the window and think, 'At least there's no volcano!'"

There is that.

I read an article that advised giving yourself permission during Thanksgiving season to not feel very grateful. I can't argue with the premise that we should feel our feelings, but is feeling ungrateful really helpful?

A different approach was chosen by my friend, who had good reason after a devastating year to not feel full of thanks. She said she was practicing "ruthless gratitude."

What a concept. It reminds me of "fierce grace," something I am all too well acquainted with. But ruthless gratitude—a deliberate and determined choice to be grateful no matter what? I had to think about that one. It reminds me of the Bible's teaching to give thanks *in* all circumstances, even when you are not grateful *for* the circumstances. Like my grandson, we can always be thankful that there's no volcano, and if there is one, we might find a way to be thankful even then.

Some years ago, I wrote a book titled *10 Steps to Finding*

Your Happy Place (and Staying There). Step 9 is: Develop an attitude of gratitude. So many studies show that gratitude is one of the easiest habits to develop and one of the most beneficial, definitely a winner in any sort of cost/benefit analysis. And gratitude, ruthless or otherwise, opens our hearts to grace.

Here is the refrain from a wonderful song about gratitude by Nimo Patel:

> *All that I am*
> *All that I see*
> *All that I've been*
> *And all that I'll ever be*
> *Is a blessing*
> *It's so amazing*
> *And I'm grateful for it all*
> *For it all*

One thing I'm grateful for is that my grandson now has a little sister who I'm sure will, over the coming years, add her own wisdom to my life.

It Does Not Touch You

Sometimes there *is* a volcano, or at least it feels like one. Someone does something or something happens that explodes your compassionate serenity. What then?

The free flow of grace is aided by good boundaries. I discovered this after someone said something to me that upset me. It was not meant to upset me, but I experienced it somewhat like an intrusion. However well intended, it felt too personal and crossed a boundary I had not even known was there.

Having heard it, I could not unhear it. For some time afterwards, it roamed around in my psyche, calling my attention to it, distracting me, disturbing me. I questioned my reaction and wondered if I could or should have handled it differently. I did not know how to resolve this in my agitated mind and release it.

And then I received a message in my spirit as clearly as if someone had spoken it aloud.

"It does not touch you."

In that moment, the truth of those words permeated my being and immediately all was well. Yes, my thoughts had been disturbed, and my emotions had been roiled. But the essence of who I am was unaffected, remaining as it is, always and forever loved, loving, pure, radiant, perfect.

Since then, this message has stayed with me. Whenever I catch myself reacting with judgment or struggling, it whispers to me, "It does not touch you." This does not mean that my heart is not touched with caring or compassion. It means that I need not feel threatened by what anyone says or does. No one has the power to harm what cannot be harmed. Rather than reacting in anger or fear, I am free to respond guided by the inner wisdom of my being.

Do I always exercise that freedom? No, of course not. However, hearing that message reminds me more quickly and more often that the choice is always mine, and mine alone.

*Nothing real can be threatened. Nothing unreal
exists. Herein lies the peace of God.*
~A Course in Miracles

The Mercy Seat

*He will cover you with his feathers, and under his
wings you will find refuge.*
~Psalm 91:4

When all else fails, pray for mercy, a prayer that is never refused regardless of to whom or what the prayer is addressed.

In the Hebrew Bible, God gives directions to Moses to build a temple. Within the temple, in the most sacred inner room, Moses is instructed to build a "mercy seat" of pure gold and to place it above the ark of the covenant. "There I will meet with you," promises God. I am no Bible scholar, so my mind is uncomplicated by specific knowledge about this seat. In my imagination, the mercy seat is the thin place where we encounter the divine (by whatever name we choose). God does not meet with us on the seat of judgment, or the seat of vengeance, but on the seat of mercy. There is no separation here, no hatred, no fear—only mercy, only grace, only love.

When I sit on the mercy seat, I am bathed in the light of divine love, filled with the basic goodness of the universe. My spirit is purified and mercy spills over like a golden fountain, flowing wherever I hold judgment and condemnation, washing away everything that is born of fear, imbuing what has been dark with a light so brilliant that nothing is left in shadow.

I hold this image in my heart when I struggle to forgive and release a situation that churns in my spirit, when I feel myself sucked back towards that whirlpool of anger, blame, fear, and pain. I picture myself on the mercy seat, opening my soul to the sacred energy that surrounds me, asking for mercy for myself and for those against whom I harbor thoughts of separation and judgment.

My prayers for mercy are often addressed to Kuan Yin, the Chinese goddess of mercy and compassion. Her name means one who hears the cries of the world. I like to think she is listening to me when I am most in need of her nectar of compassion. When I cry out for her help, I feel enveloped in her sacred robes, held in her gentle embrace, perfectly and profoundly loved.

Imagining myself on the golden seat of mercy is humbling. The true gift of grace is that mercy never flows in only one direction. The line between giving and receiving mercy disappears as soon as mercy is asked for or offered, and compassion washes over everyone. When I am on the mercy seat, I am not only forgiven, but forgiveness flows easily to others. Grace is so exquisite, the limitless generosity of the Universe so sublime, that my grievances simply melt away. I am bewildered that I ever thought them important, worthy of my attention and energy. What are they compared to this glorious liberation from what entraps my soul?

Blessed are the merciful, for they shall receive mercy.
~Matthew 5:7

At the Gate

There is a place
Of perfect peace
Not a place of our own making
No need to make what already is
No need to fix what is unbroken
Where is this place
If you look you will not see it
If you seek you will not find it
But if you ask
It will find you

One of my favorite movies is *King of Hearts*, a 1960s film starring Alan Bates and Geneviève Bujold. The story takes place in a village in France during WWI. The inhabitants flee the town to escape the advancing German army, leaving behind the inmates of an asylum with the gate open. The inmates filter out into the empty town and take on the roles of normal life, full of joie de vivre. A lone Scottish soldier (Bates) is sent into the town on a mission unaware of the situation, with hilarious and profound results.

This brief description does no justice to this gem of a movie but sets the stage for the final scene. After opposing armies meet and kill each other in the town square, the inmates realize that the villagers will be returning. They quietly abandon their adventure and return to the asylum. Finally understanding what has happened, Bates reluctantly rejoins his unit and prepares to move out. But at the very end, he returns and walks towards the asylum, shedding his uniform along the way, until he stands before the gate, stark naked, asking to be admitted.

The people we find most appealing in the movie are those who have been judged insane—the ones who appreciate life, reveling in the present moment with open hearts and flashes of deep wisdom. When confronted by the dismal reality of the life he had never questioned up to that moment, Bates, along with the viewer, is led to consider that the inmates of the asylum might understand more about the precious nature of life than those who so thoughtlessly cast it aside.

His walk towards the gate, to me, represents the process of awakening. When we shed our attachments and release our aversions, the beauty and interconnectedness of creation are revealed and we see that we are safe at home, where we've always been, showered with endless grace. It requires utter surrender, leaving behind everything we use to clothe ourselves: our beliefs, our judgments, our shame, our stories, our hopes, our fears. We must be willing to let it all go, layer by layer, like the uniform left strewn behind him, until we stand at the door naked, with nothing to offer except ourselves, asking to come in.

And we will be welcomed, because we are standing at the gate of home.

Ask and it will be given to you; seek and you will find; knock and the door will be opened to you.
~Matthew 7:7

Abiding in Tenderness

Mind has determined, "Reason comes to this point and can go no further."

Love does not even see the barrier. When Love crashes through mind's familiar understanding of how things ought to be, mind can only cry out, "That's a miracle!"

"No," Love answers, "that's just the way I am."
~Emmanuel's Book III

When we fold up our umbrellas of fear and allow the eternal shower of grace to rain upon us, we find ourselves living in peaceful contentment. When asked about his personal path, Sifu Adam Mizner listed several aspects, the first being "abiding." What he meant, he explained, was a quality of empty knowing, leading to freedom, awakening, and liberation.

Abiding. What a great word. When I looked up the etymology, I found a reference to "waiting onwards." This is not the impatient waiting while we are on hold listening to annoying music and recorded announcements about how important our call is. This is the pregnant waiting of possibility, curiosity, innocence, trust.

One of my favorite lines in the *Dao De Jing* counsels us to "abide in tenderness." When we abide in tenderness, we are at peace, trusting the Universe, confident in our inner guidance. We are showered with grace that bathes our spirit and spills over to everything and everyone around us.

What is the secret to abiding in tenderness? This question is often answered with murky messages about looking within. And of course that is true. But there is one very concrete, unambiguous answer I've found, one that we've already looked at and that bears repeating. Adyashanti said, "The price of awakening is giving up every reason you have to stop loving." Awakening is what opens up the spirit to abiding in tenderness.

So all I have to do is give up all the reasons I have to stop loving? No problem. Except for that one jerk that ruined my life. Or the kid who was mean to me in school. Or the friend who ghosted me.

Every reason? Really? Yes. Every reason. Really. The price of awakening sometimes seems too steep. That's what price means, though. We have to want something more than what we have to give up to get it. And when we do want something that much, the price is paid willingly.

Abiding in tenderness isn't something we "do" as much as it is something we experience. It is a quality of grace, received rather than attained, received when we surrender everything that blocks its blessing. So wait onward, knowing that you are cherished just as you are, liberated, free, beloved.

We think ourselves unworthy
Always falling short
Damned by fatal flaws
We have forgotten who we are
Beloved children all
Of the Divine Mother

Ever held as babes
In her sacred embrace
Rocked in her arms
To the rhythm of her heart
Listening as she sings away
Our dreams of separation
Gazing into her eyes of grace
Reflecting back to us
Our own perfection

CHAPTER 6

The Dance of Synchronicity

When you stop existing and you start truly living,
each moment of the day comes alive with wonder
and synchronicity.
~Steve Maraboli

There is a marvelous quality to our ordinary lives when we surrender in trust to the grace that flows ever present. This quality might be described as synchronicity, an experience of everything being connected, moving naturally and effortlessly in harmony. We see through the illusion of conflict and embrace everything that arises within the sphere of our awareness. We are at peace in the center of the ups and downs of daily life as we dance gracefully and fluidly to the heartbeat of creation.

Releasing the Illusion of Conflict

We cannot hear the music of the dance until we recognize and release the illusion of conflict.

> *Fighting will never bring peace*
> *Ceasing to fight will never bring peace*
> *Only ceasing to fear will bring peace*
> *We will cease to fear*
>   *when we realize there is nothing to fear*

We will realize there is nothing to fear
when we remember who we are
We will remember who we are
when we release everything we are not
We will release everything we are not
when we understand that everything we are not is ...
Everything

A Divided World

The world is divided into people
who think they are right.
~Tara Brach

When I first read this quote, it took me a few seconds to understand that this was a complete sentence. Each side of the divide claims the higher ground of being right, being righteous, being morally superior, being more ethical, being smarter, being better.

This was evident to me in the news stories of two business owners, one liberal and one conservative, each of whom denied service to a customer based on the owner's sense of morality. The liberal business owner denied service to a conservative politician. The conservative business owner denied service to a gay couple. The customers in both cases were denied service because of who they were thought to be, not because they were engaged in any behavior disruptive to the businesses in question.

I'm not going to debate the legalities, the politics, or any other aspect of the owners' decisions. What caught my attention was the public reaction to these similar decisions to deny service. Liberals condemned the refusal of service to the gay couple while praising the refusal to serve a conservative politician. Conservatives condemned the refusal of service to the politician while praising the refusal to serve a gay couple.

Neither group seemed to see any contradiction in their own opposite reactions to basically the same scenario. And of course each group saw their reaction as the "right" one. But how can any of this be right? How can any of this lead to anything other than more distrust, more judgment, more hatred, more insistence, more fighting, more of everything that divides us as human beings?

Sometimes all I can do is pray: Kuan Yin, goddess of mercy and compassion, please pour your nectar of compassion over all of us, over both business owners, over both customers, over all who have furthered the divide, and over all who seek to bridge it. Help us love with the love that we profess to believe in, help us open our hearts to receive the ever present grace we long for, help us reach through our fear to find a hand reaching out from the other side. May we see that our conflict is never with an "other," but always within ourselves.

> *Conflict arises when illusions birthed from fearful perceptions are entertained.*
> ~Hope Forsythe Newell

Friend or Foe

Our mistaken belief in a divided world is rooted in our basic world view. As noted earlier, Einstein said that the most important decision we make is whether we believe we live in a friendly or hostile universe. We hold so much power to create the world we experience, and most of us don't even know it. We mistake our lens of judgment for objective reality and fall victim to it. And of course, once we make that initial decision about the universe, then we see what reinforces it.

A quick exploration of YouTube videos demonstrates this. When I click on typical news stories—often about politics, war, mass shootings—I feel a sense of frustration or despair. On the other hand, if I click on stories of random acts of kindness, I feel uplifted and grateful, and inspired to look for opportunities to be kind. How can I reconcile the two visions of the universe represented in these videos, one friendly and the other hostile? Do I believe in one only by denying evidence of the other? Are they mutually exclusive or can one include the other? Can I choose to believe in a benign universe while acknowledging everything and denying nothing?

Perhaps my choice of lens is not about selective seeing and denying, but rather about orientation or perspective. If I choose to believe that I live in a friendly universe, then can I see everyone and everything in a way that connects rather than divides? When I view my world through this lens, then actions that I find indefensible evoke not outrage, but compassion.

A friendly universe can hold it all, including everything and everyone. A friendly universe is a gift we give ourselves, a gift of an open heart, released from conflict, at peace in the midst of protest, at one with all creation.

> *I can choose to see this differently.*
> ~A Course in Miracles

The Enemy Is Me!

> *Yesterday I was clever, so I wanted to change the world. Today I am wise, so I am changing myself.*
> ~Rumi

Sometimes we are the ones creating division even as we think we are seeking to correct it. I began a blog post once with Pogo's quote "We have seen the enemy, and he is us." The post was about a person who canceled a holiday party to avoid inviting people who voted for the presidential candidate he voted against. I noted the irony of discriminating against people because they voted for someone who discriminates, and ended the post by saying that the person who canceled the party was welcome at my table, along with those who voted for the other guy.

A friend later commented that the post was "morally smug in its own way, which is how I believe you characterized" the guy who canceled the party.

What? Me? You mean that while I'm pointing out the irony of someone judging others for voting for someone who judges others, I myself am judging? That while I am calling someone out for smugly excluding others, I am smugly including everyone? Is that any different? *A Course in Miracles* says that we teach what we want to learn. In my frustration and sadness over the rancor splitting up friends, neighbors, and families, I tried to pluck the speck from my brother's eye, while overlooking the log in my own.

Furthermore, my friend asked if I would really welcome everyone to my table. Well, okay, I wouldn't literally sit down with a serial killer. So how is that different from not sitting down with people who don't agree with my political views?

I don't have a good answer to that, except that in the physical world, and even in the emotional world, good boundaries are healthy, and in extreme cases even necessary for survival. But in the realm of spirit, boundaries have a different impact. They block us from sacred union, which is what our spirits yearn for. If we can keep our heart doors open, then perhaps our understanding and compassion can lead to expanded connection, even as we maintain healthy boundaries.

The best example I can think of is an Amish community that refused to hate the man who came into one of their schools and shot ten young girls, killing five of them, before killing himself. One author said that, had the killer not died on the scene, the community would have supported whatever consequences the law imposed and then visited him in prison. Their example lit up the news around the world, and the story became not only one of soul crushing tragedy, but also one of soul lifting beauty.

So my challenge is to keep my heart open, to welcome, yes truly welcome, everyone to my heart table, if not to my literal table. For example, instead of judging, I might have practiced compassion for the person who decided who was welcome and not welcome at his table. And having myself judged him, I had an opportunity to practice compassion for myself.

Thanks to the friend who held up a mirror to help me see where my own work lies.

It's here
Right here
Oh look again
If you could see
All war would cease
For why would we fight
Our own reflection
So look again
Do you not see
Yourself
In every face you fear
So who then is your enemy
Please look again
Until you see
The face of God
For none else exists

Two Become One

Sometimes a visual helps us see through the illusion of conflict. We saw this yin yang symbol in Chapter 4. Yin and yang are sometimes thought of as opposites. Rather than opposites, however, the symbol reveals the complementary wholeness of the circle as the two shapes eternally flow one into the other. This is emphasized by the small dots, a light dot in the darker shape and a dark dot in the lighter shape, showing that the essence of each is contained in the other.

Nature reflects this in the seasons. The first day of summer is the longest day of the year. As summer progresses, however, the days get shorter, heralding the coming winter. Conversely, as we enter the cold, rainy months of winter, each day is getting longer, promising that summer will come again. Likewise, joy and sadness cycle in their turn, yet each is part of the whole process of opening the heart. Even our breath reflects this, as each inhale and exhale flow in rhythmic exchange of oxygen and carbon dioxide, an exchange mirrored in the plant world.

When faced with an apparent conflict, this yin yang symbol helps me shift from a stuck adversarial perspective. It teaches me to look for the movement of complementary ideas, each reflecting some common value. Instead of using force against force, yielding allows the cycle to turn, creating openings for other ideas naturally to emerge.

I once witnessed two parents arguing about whether their water-averse child should take swimming lessons. One parent felt that the child should not be forced to swim, while the other parent felt that lessons would help the child become comfortable in the water. They thought they were stuck in conflicting positions.

Yet with further exploration, both parents realized they agreed on key points. They both loved their child, both wanted their child to be comfortable in the water, and neither believed that forcing the child into the water was the way to achieve this. Recognizing their common ground, they agreed to provide opportunities for the child to be around water with a skilled teacher who could (hopefully) gradually and gently help the child learn to enjoy the water. There never really was a conflict.

And really, there never is.

The ten thousand things carry yin and embrace yang.
They achieve harmony by combining these forces.
~Dao De Jing

Deflecting Conflict

Martial arts has taught me much about the illusion of conflict. A visiting teacher instructed us to be nice, be generous, and be patient. We might imagine that this advice would leave us weak or vulnerable. However, she demonstrated the wisdom and power of this instruction, repeatedly taking down bigger, stronger opponents.

By being nice, she meant that aggressive force often leads to defeat because there is always someone stronger. Instead, she turned the attacker's own force back towards him in response. If an attacker wanted to move in a certain direction or occupy a certain space, the teacher generously yielded and strategically moved into unclaimed and more advantageous space, sometimes saying something like, "Oh, you want this space? Okay take it." If an attacker took hold of her in some way, instead of trying to escape the hold immediately, she would be still and patiently wait to see what the attacker would do, at which point...see the examples of being nice and being generous above.

Life gives me many opportunities to practice what I learn in martial arts. Once I was walking along a neighborhood street after dark. Up ahead was a group of teenage boys. As I passed them, one of them said something vulgar to me, intending to incite anger or fear. When I walked past without reacting, they fell in behind me and started to follow.

I assessed the situation. There was no one else on the street and they were coming up close behind me. So I did what any self-respecting martial artist would do and turned to face them. I gave them all a big smile and said to the young man in front who had spoken to me, "When an old lady like me gets a compliment from a handsome young fella like yourself, it's a good day!" Then I stood there grinning and waited.

They weren't expecting that! They all stopped in their tracks and looked confused. Then the one who had spoken to me softened his stance and simply said, "God bless you."

"God bless you too," I replied.

All the tension evaporated. We all nodded at each other, turned, and went on our way.

We can't always stop someone from saying something unkind or treating us with disrespect. People might even approach us in a threatening way. Reacting in fear, or trying to overpower someone with forceful words or physical behavior, can escalate the situation. Staying centered and open allows us to respond in the best way possible, whatever that might be.

Be kind whenever possible. It is always possible.
~The Dalai Lama

When We Walked with God

Some of us can trace our concept of conflict back a very long way. The Garden of Eden story fascinates me. Just for a moment, consider the story itself without any additional religious or Biblical context.

Adam and Eve lived in this beautiful place, where they had a life of ease, with plenty of food. The weather must have been pleasant because they were without clothing. They walked in the garden with God, in whose image they were created. There were many trees in this garden paradise, but only two were named: the tree of life, and the tree of knowledge of good and evil. The people were free to eat the fruit of any tree, presumably including the tree of life, but they were warned not to eat from the tree of knowledge of good and evil, for if they did, they would "surely die."

Why did these two trees stand in contrast to each other? The fruit from the tree of life bestowed immortality, but the fruit from the tree of knowledge of good and evil promised death. What is it about the knowledge of good and evil that is incompatible with life? It might be easier to understand if the forbidden tree was the tree of evil. But it seems like *knowing* the difference between good and evil would be a good thing. Why wasn't it?

One way to think about it might be that knowledge of good and evil created duality. Before this knowledge, Adam and Eve lived in unselfconscious harmony with God. But what was the first thing that happened after they ate the forbidden fruit? They became aware that they were naked, and they were ashamed. They tried to cover themselves up literally, with leaves. And figuratively, they tried to cover up what they had done by hiding from God.

In effect, they became self-conscious in a way they weren't before, and perceived themselves as separate from God, which caused them to be afraid. And they suffered, not because they had done something evil, but because they had stepped out of alignment with the natural harmony of life. They had, in essence, forgotten who they were.

When we are living in harmony, opposing concepts of goodness/evil, kindness/cruelty, and justice/injustice are meaningless, because harmony transcends conflict. Everything in the dance of synchronicity happens naturally and without effort. There is nothing to fear because there is acceptance of *what is* without struggle. There is acceptance without fear and without struggle because we are integrated naturally and harmoniously with what is. We *are* what is. We can be nothing else. When we remember who we are, we are restored to the garden to walk again with God.

> *Know thyself.*
> ~Oracle at Delphi

Entering the Dance

Like with any new dance, we might feel awkward at first until gradually we begin to move naturally in harmony with the rhythm of our lives. As we surrender to the music of our souls, the Universe leads us in the dance of creation.

> *Synchronicity spontaneously emerges out of*
> *a void of nothingness, which brings the magic*
> *of the universe to life.*
> ~Jason Gregory

The Dance of Release

A life in harmony with the music of our souls is effortless, without conflict or strife. So when someone asked me if struggle is how we grow spiritually, I responded that struggle is not *how* we grow; it's *where* we grow. *How* we grow is by releasing the struggle. The dance of synchronicity is often a dance of release.

I like the phrase "the razor's edge of practice." This is where I am poised on a challenge, something that has the potential to get me hooked, something that triggers an urge to grasp or reject or control. The razor's edge is where I have a choice about which side I'm going to step into: the side of fear and struggle, or the side of trust and effortlessness. Where that edge is, is different for different people. And different for the same person at different times. Whether we find ourselves on this edge repeatedly or rarely ever, it is always an opportunity to make the choice to struggle or to release.

When I choose to step into struggle, I feel it throughout my body. I tense up, my breathing moves up into my chest, and I am caught in my thinking mind. No need to judge myself. Instead, I let the breath sink into my belly. Because struggle almost always involves fear at some level, I try to tolerate the discomfort and uncertainty long enough to go into the center of the struggle to find the fear. When I embrace the fear with understanding and compassion, the fear softens. I can then release the struggle and allow the natural flow of energy to resume.

The dance continues. In this moment...and this one....

You only struggle because you're ready to grow but
aren't willing to let go.
~Drew Gerald

Life's Basic Training

Learning to dance doesn't mean that there will not be challenges. At a meditation class, I was paired up with a young man for a time of sharing reflections. He told me the following story.

When he was 19, he joined the military. During basic training, the drill sergeant would find some mistake every morning during inspection and make his group do push-ups as a consequence. Maybe a bed was not made properly, or shoes were not polished, or someone was a nanosecond too slow in obeying an order. Every day they would strive mightily for perfection, fail, and drop to the ground in frustration to perform what they saw as penalty push-ups.

Finally, he realized that the point of this pattern was not the daily mistake; the point was the daily push-ups. The drill sergeant would find some reason for push-ups every day no matter what they did or didn't do. He began to view the push-ups not as punishment but as exercise, difficult exercise, yes, but exercise that was part of their training. The push-ups were the same, but his experience of the push-ups changed. He said that he suffered less than others in his group who still tried to attain that magic perfection that would avoid the ordered push-ups.

His story illustrates life's basic training. We strive for an ever elusive perfection that will avoid challenge, disappointment, distress, heartache. If I learn to meditate better, I will always be peaceful. If I practice martial arts long enough, I will never be afraid. If I pray hard enough, my prayers will be answered according to my wishes. If I love wisely, my heart will never be broken.

But here is life's reality. I may be fidgety during meditation. I may feel frustrated when I don't handle situations as well as I would like. I may feel embarrassed by something I did. I may feel disappointed when I had hoped for something different. I may feel sad when I lose something important to me. I may feel angry when I perceive being wronged.

Yes, there will be push-ups. I can struggle to avoid them but I will fail. I can judge myself as lacking and the consequences as punishment. Or I can see the push-ups as a part of life, weaving them into a tapestry full of experiences and opportunities.

A moment of radical acceptance is a moment of genuine freedom.
~Tara Brach

The Dance Is Always Perfect

People sometimes think that when you live an awakened life, you are always serene, always giddily happy, always wise. But that's not true. Spiritual awakening is not a one-time thing. As Adyashanti says, there is no such thing as enlightenment. There are only enlightened moments, because enlightenment, or awakening, can only happen in this moment. And this one. In other words, the dance is dynamic and ongoing.

Enlightened moments are those in which we are fully engaged with what is, directly experiencing the present moment, without the filter of our judgments and stories about what is happening, without the desire to hold on to or change or avoid reality, without the illusory refuge of alternative facts. Instead, in enlightened moments, we realize and accept that what is, simply *is*.

Enlightened moments are not always serene. Sometimes what is happening is hard, or sad, or unpleasant. We might have a range of feelings, including some we might label as "bad." I can try to deny such a feeling and hide it, especially from myself, or try to transform it into something more lofty, more spiritually acceptable. Or I can just let it be, knowing that without adding energy to it through struggle, it will soon dissolve on its own. I need not express it outwardly towards others, but I can acknowledge it with compassion and hold it tenderly until it is soothed.

Our notions of how we "should" act, our efforts to mold ourselves into some ideal of an enlightened person, our judgments of how we always fall short, are all harmful to ourselves by perpetuating the very separation that we seek to heal. Awakening begins at home, with self-acceptance. What we yearn for is right here, in this moment, in plain view if we look with unclouded eyes and embrace what we see with the arms of compassion. And while the dance might not always be serene, it is always perfect.

> *I am what I am, and that's all that I am.*
> ~Popeye the Sailor Man

Dancing with Whoever Shows Up

> *This being human is a guest house.*
> *Every morning a new arrival.*
> *A joy, a depression, a meanness,*
> *some momentary awareness*
> *comes as an unexpected visitor.*
> *Welcome and entertain them all!*
> *Even if they're a crowd of sorrows,*
> *who violently sweep your house*
> *empty of its furniture,*
> *still, treat each guest honorably.*
> *He may be clearing you out for some new delight.*

The dark thought, the shame, the malice,
meet them at the door laughing, and invite them in.
Be grateful for whoever comes,
because each has been sent
as a guide from beyond.
~Rumi

This poem came as a guest into my life after a series of events left me at various times elated, terrified, energized, devastated, regretful, confused, excited, upset, exhausted, stunned, content, happy, and lost. This poem knocked on my door and offered me a framework for holding all these events and feelings in my heart with gratitude.

"Each has been sent as a guide from beyond." That's a comforting and encouraging way to view things, isn't it? Each guide comes bearing a gift, if I'm willing to receive it. Every experience, the pleasant and the brutal, has something to teach me, to reveal to me. Guiding me towards ... what? Something profound? Dare I hope?

Perhaps nothing so grand. Perhaps putting our welcome mat out for whoever or whatever stops by leads us towards the simple acceptance of what is. We cease to judge. We cease to struggle or resist. We cease to grasp and try to hold on. We make our peace and fall in love with life. All of it. This is true for whatever form the "guest" takes: a person, a situation, even our own thoughts and emotions. Perhaps especially our own thoughts and emotions.

The Buddhist story is told of Milarepa, who came back to his cave one day to find it filled with demons. He didn't know how to get rid of them. He got angry and attacked them. They just laughed. He tried to teach them Buddhism. They ignored him. Finally, he gave up and said, "I'm not going anywhere, and it seems that you are not either. I guess we will have to live here together. Let's have some tea."

The story says that upon Milarepa's offer of hospitality, the demons promptly disappeared, but I wonder. Perhaps they stayed, along with the neighbors, artists, pets, politicians, dust bunnies, laughing children, kings, beggars, lost lovers, birth, death, and everything in between—all guides from beyond welcomed in Milarepa's guest house. At least long enough to enjoy some tea.

> *Synchronicity is an ever present reality for those who have eyes to see.*
> ~Carl Jung

The Cost of Freedom

> *Find the cost of freedom*
> *Buried in the ground*
> *Mother Earth will swallow you*
> *Lay your body down*
> ~Stephen Stills

As we learn to dance more joyfully, more freely, we realize that there is a price for liberation. There was a time when for several days, I awoke humming the song's refrain about the cost of freedom, and it replayed throughout the day and rocked me to sleep. Although it was written about war, it sang to my soul about internal war, the one we fight with ourselves.

The First Noble Truth of Buddhism teaches that human existence is suffering. We suffer because we struggle. We desire things, including ourselves, to be other than they are and we fight to make them conform to our wishes. We fight until we learn that resistance is futile.

A series of seemingly unrelated events over a period of a couple of years brought me repeatedly to the razor's edge, the place where we practice. With each event, I went through the same process of struggle, acceptance, and peace. Then I would sit smugly in relief, thinking that surely I had passed all my cosmic tests. But the Universe, in its infinite wisdom and with a warped sense of humor, would nod and say, "Okay, well then how about this?" And off we'd go again.

Marianne Williamson wrote about a series of events in her own life that kept knocking her to her knees. With that good old perseverance that we value so much in our culture, she would pull herself to her feet only to be knocked down again. Finally, she realized maybe she should just stay on her knees.

"Surrender is the name of the spiritual game," teaches Adyashanti. And so it is. Not the surrender of defeat, but the surrender into freedom. I saw that my struggle to avoid pain and uncertainty was a struggle masking grief and sadness with anger and frustration, a struggle not born of courage but of fear.

In that instantaneous way we sometimes realize the simplest and most obvious things, I saw that I didn't need to struggle anymore. I…could…just…stop. I could lay my body down to be swallowed up in the loving arms of the Universe. I could choose freedom. And so I did. And so I do, again and again. Freedom is a choice available to all of us in every moment, with every breath. The cost? Taking full responsibility for your life.

> *I will fight no more forever.*
> ~Chief Joseph

> *Well, at least for today.*
> ~me

Dancing Like Water

When we release the illusion of conflict and enter the dance, we are fluid rather than rigid in our lives. We can flow with the current of life and dance freely with creation. Water is the image most often used as a metaphor for the movement of energy in the universe. This energy creates us, flows through our lives, and carries us home.

> *Be water, my friend.*
> ~Bruce Lee

What Would Water Do

Water's wisdom is its ability to respond effortlessly and appropriately to any situation. It flows around obstacles. It yields to force (think about trying to push water). It flows downhill in harmony with gravity. It takes the shape of whatever contains it. When there is nowhere to go, it rests in tranquility. It transforms in response to heat or cold. It fills the lowest places, yet nothing is more powerful. It nourishes all life without judgment or striving. And it returns to the sea. The Chinese character for sea or ocean is 海, which breaks down into "water mother." The *Dao De Jing* describes the Dao using many characters and references that relate to water. It compares the Dao's presence in the world to streams flowing through nurturing valleys into rivers and back home to the sea.

We are made mostly of water (with a sprinkling of stardust), so it is our nature to move through our lives effortlessly, and ultimately to return to our source. We don't need to "do" anything. Like swimming upstream, our efforts slow us down, but will not keep us from our destiny. Like water, we need only "allow."

Water is the original practitioner of the dance of synchronicity. When I find myself stuck or struggling, I remember the phrase: WWJD—What Would Jesus Do? I've adapted it to water: WWWD—What Would Water Do? As we go through our day, we can listen to water's wisdom, for indeed it is our own. When facing a challenge, or unsure what to do, we can pause and ask ourselves, "What would water do?" Trust your innate wisdom to respond appropriately.

> *Don't push the river. It flows by itself.*
> ~Fritz Perls

Water Moves the Color

> *I am open to the guidance of synchronicity, and do*
> *not let expectations hinder my path.*
> ~The Dalai Lama

We can learn about water's wisdom by directly engaging with it. I once participated in an art and meditation workshop. That may not sound like such a remarkable thing unless you know that I feel about a blank piece of art paper the way some people feel about a blank screen when they are trying to write. So if you really understand how reluctant I am to do anything even remotely artistic, you will marvel at my willingness to try out this workshop. The meditation aspect of the art and meditation workshop was the hook—meditation I'm comfortable with, and so I went.

The director of the workshop began with all of us in a sitting area. So far so good. I can sit. Tables and shelves in another part of the room were filled with all kinds of art supplies. Her presence was calming, and she assured us that this workshop was not about producing a certain product using specific techniques. It was about exploring, playing, discovering, allowing. My mind heard "blah, blah, blah" as anxiety nipped at my heels.

Then, in giving us a brief orientation to the watercolor materials, she used the phrase "Water moves the color." As we settled into meditation, those words held out their hands, inviting me to dance. After a period of silence, we moved into the art area. I felt excited and a tiny bit brave. I picked a large piece of watercolor paper taped to a board. I closed my eyes and moved my hands over the paper; it wasn't as scary when I didn't look. I opened my eyes long enough to chose a few colors and squeezed the paint out beside the paper.

No brushes, I decided. Just my hands, water, and color. I cupped my hands into the water container and soaked the paper until it was saturated. Then I stuck my hands in the paint, closed my eyes again, and let my fingers dance in the puddles. And guess what … water moved the color! Little rainbow rivulets flowed across the ridges and into the valleys created by the wet paper. I watched with fascination. But the water wasn't done. Gradually, as the paint and paper dried, shapes and lines emerged that could not have been predicted. It was like the water itself was painting, and I was simply a witness to its own creative dynamic. It was all a beautiful surprise, one I neither envisioned nor controlled.

Without a specific plan, I surrendered control and let the paint move with the water. I felt liberated. I was curious and amazed. I had fun. I was dancing with the water and something beautiful emerged.

This works much the same way in life. When I approach a situation with curiosity rather than a preconceived idea of a particular outcome, when I allow things to unfold naturally, the outcome is often not what I would have predicted. No matter what it is, I have a sense that it is perfect as it is, and I am at peace. As Larry Eisenberg said, for peace of mind resign as general manager of the universe!

Everything Is Part of the Dance

As life invites us to move in harmony with all of creation, the sphere of our experience can expand to include the entire range of existence. The *Avatamsaka Sutra* describes the "jeweled net of Indra" as representing the interconnectedness of the universe. This net stretches to infinity in all directions. A jewel is placed at each intersection of webbing, likewise infinite in number. Each facet of each jewel reflects all the other jewels in the net. And within each reflection is reflected all the other jewels and all the other reflections, thus creating a dynamic phenomenon of infinite reflection.

Like the jewels in Indra's net, we are, in the most profound and fundamental way, truly all in this together. *A Course in Miracles* teaches that there is no individual enlightenment, that we awaken together. Like good Marines, we leave no one behind.

The largest living organism on the planet is a mushroom fungus in eastern Oregon that covers many square miles. The fungus is a web of filaments under the ground. What we think of as mushrooms are actually the fruits of the fungus, sprouting up here and there above the ground, yet all connected under the surface.

Like us. We are all individual expressions of the single organism of creation. We are never really separate, and everything we do generates energy that affects everything else. Our breath is the simplest evidence of this intimate connection. Breath links us one to the other like Indra's jeweled net. Sometimes when I'm at my cabin in the mountains, I relax in a hammock strung between two majestic trees. As I lie in the hammock, I experience the exchange of oxygen and carbon dioxide as I breathe in symbiotic rhythm with the trees.

All life is reflected in me, and I am reflected by all life. I breathe all life and all life breathes me.

Our individual separateness is in a sense illusory…our minds are the fitful flashes of eternal light.
~Will Durant

Living the Dance of Synchronicity

Synchronicity brings together occurrences that might seem unrelated, like two strangers drawn to one another on the dance floor where they enter the current of other dancers. The music moves everyone in harmony, the dancers yielding to and carried by the vibration that resonates universally and individually. The music connects all the random people who have stepped onto the dance floor.

The word "synchronicity," coined by Carl Jung in the 1950s to describe a meaningful relationship or connection between apparent coincidences, combines the roots of "together" and "time." I like the sound of synchronicity when I say it out loud. It has a catchy rhythm that moves like a dance in my mouth.

Life is a dance of synchronicity, everything connected, everything affecting every other thing. Some of the effects we recognize, like environmental causes for climate change. Other effects may be more subtle yet no less profound, like a small kindness with far reaching ripple effects.

When we are attuned to the natural rhythm of the universe, we move effortlessly, in harmony with the current of the cosmos, in step with the music of the spheres. We feel it. We also sense when we are "out of sync." Most of us experience that from time to time, or perhaps often. When that happens, we can't think or force our way back into attunement. But when we listen, we can hear the song of our soul. When we yield, we will be guided. When we surrender, we will be carried. We open ourselves to experience the connection with all life in the dance of synchronicity.

> *In every moment, the Universe is whispering to you.*
> *You're constantly surrounded by signs, coincidences,*
> *and synchronicities, all aimed at propelling you in the*
> *direction of your destiny.*
> ~Denise Linn

CHAPTER 7

Destiny Is All

Let love carry you where it will
Along the currents of the vast universe
Countless marvels to behold
Do not struggle
Fear will not keep you from your destiny
But you will miss the splendor
Of this precious life

If you are a fan of *The Last Kingdom*, you will recognize the "destiny is all" tag line. Destiny is a powerful word. It comes from a Latin word meaning to make firm or to establish. The word is used and abused in all sorts of contexts: religious, political, and personal. But I use it here to mean a universal life purpose. When we listen for its call and heed it, we have a sense of alignment and "rightness." We are part of something bigger than ourselves, something infinite and mysterious.

Our destiny might not be what we think it is. We might think in terms of career perhaps, or a specific life purpose. For example, a friend tells me her destiny is to be a witness to truth. Another friend often bemoans her lack of purpose, when all along I see how she tends to everyone she meets with kindness and generosity of spirit. It is her calling, whether or not she can see its priceless value.

Going deeper, however, destiny is something more fundamental. Whatever our life circumstances and choices, there is a deep river of destiny that runs through our souls, seeking to manifest. We don't need to be trained for it; we need only allow it and trust it. We hear its call in the quietness of our spirit when we listen, really listen, with our whole selves. We recognize it by the opening of our hearts. Destiny does not isolate or fear, but rather expands and embraces. Through it, we are connected to all creation.

Even as we live enlightened moments, however, showered with grace, dancing in synchronicity, our egos still occasionally seek validation. Am I making progress? How do I know? Am I further along than that person over there? Like the restless, impatient kids in the back seat, we sometimes pester ourselves with the question, "Am I there yet?" We might recognize some of these "stages of awakening" in ourselves:

I Want It

The allure of awakening has caught our attention and we set out with determination to attain it. We read books, go to workshops, find a teacher, find a different teacher, listen to podcasts, buy a beautiful meditation cushion, chant mantras, pray with mala beads. We are drawn to anyone or anything that sets out clear steps to follow, with the assurance that we will reach our goal.

I'll Never Get It

After an initial period of enthusiastic dedication, we begin to tire. How long does this take? Is there a faster way? What am I doing wrong? It sometimes feels like we are getting further away rather than closer. We begin to despair.

I Got It!

We have a grand spiritual experience and laugh/cry with ecstasy and relief that we finally made it. We have arrived. Smooth sailing on the sea of serenity from here on out.

I Lost It

Oh no! Despite our efforts to hold on to our moment of blissful awareness, it slips through our fingers. Where did it go? How do I get it back? We try to recreate the experience…and fail.

I Never Had It

Doubt sets in. If it was real, it would have lasted. I wouldn't be feeling this way again. I would do better, be better. I would never have these problems anymore. Maybe I just made it up. I must not have awakened after all.

I've Always Had It

We begin to understand that awakening isn't something we attain. It is our true nature, our essential being. I don't have to do anything or be anything. No one can give it to me or take it away. I can't lose it. It is closer than my breath, the life force in every cell, the energy of creation we all share, connecting all aspects of existence to each other and to the source. It is what is. That's all.

All destinies, while appearing in different forms in each of us, are in essence one destiny. Destiny sends us out from the origin of heaven and earth to bring forth the beauty of the garden into this world, to awaken from the dream of separation, to reach across and open the way.

We breathe our destiny with every breath. Receive each breath with gratitude. Your breath is a precious gift. You are a precious gift. You are not here by accident. You are not a mistake. You are a masterpiece, created in beauty and called to manifest your destiny. We need not be concerned about success or failure. Our very existence manifests our destiny. It is who we are. One cosmic expansion of Being. We cannot be other. So it is. And so we relax into these last stages:

It Doesn't Matter

"Before enlightenment chop wood carry water. After enlightenment chop wood carry water." We practice because we practice. We breathe because we breathe. We love because we love. We are here, now. There is nowhere else we can be. There is no other time than this moment. Occasionally I am aware of that. Sometimes I'm not. Either way, I am still here, now.

Have Some Tea

So make some tea and welcome whoever and whatever shows up at your table. Keep the water hot. More will surely come.

The ground beneath our feet
That we think strong
Is but an icy crust
Lightning cracks race
Pop and thunder
We dare not move
It matters not
We will fall through
Into our destiny
And remember once again
That what dies
Was never real
And we are
> *Laughing*
> *Free*

One love, one heart, one destiny.
~Bob Marley

Breathing in, I smile. Breathing out, I release.
Breathing in, I dwell in the present moment.
Breathing out, I feel it is a wonderful moment.
~Thich Nhat Hanh

Acknowledgments

I did not include an acknowledgment page in my previous books, not because I had no one to thank, but because of the opposite: there were so many people to thank I couldn't list them all. The same is certainly true of this book as well. Even so, with apologies to those to whom I'm so indebted but are too numerous to name, there are three whose help was essential to making this book a reality: Liz, the editor who turned a sow's ear into a silk purse; Marjorie, the proofreader who bedazzled the purse; and Vinnie, the project manager who has made all three of my books look exquisitely beautiful regardless of the content. I bow in gratitude to you and to all the others who have encouraged me and supported me and loved me through this process.

Galen Pearl is a spiritual director, guide, teacher and student, martial artist, writer, retired law professor, explorer of the *Dao De Jing* and other wisdom teachings, and embracer of life's mystery. When she is not leading her monthly contemplation group, practicing with her martial arts buddies, or playing with her grandchildren, you can usually find her sitting by the creek at her forest cabin in the mountains.